BEVERLEY MINSTER, FROM THE RAILWAY STATION.

Frontispiece: Beverley Minster from the railway station.
(J. J. Sheahan, **Green's** *... **hand-book to Beverley**, c. 1875)*

BEVERLEY
IN MID-VICTORIAN
TIMES

by

Jan Crowther

HUTTON PRESS
1990

Published by

The Hutton Press Ltd.
130 Canada Drive, Cherry Burton
Beverley, East Yorkshire HU17 7SB

Printed and bound by

Clifford Ward & Co. (Bridlington) Ltd.
55 West Street, Bridlington, East Yorkshire
YO15 3DZ

ISBN 1 872167 03 9

CONTENTS

PREFACE

This attempt to paint a picture of daily life in Beverley in mid-Victorian times arose out of research undertaken by a University of Hull/Workers' Educational Association local history class which began in 1984. We should like to thank all past members of the class for their contributions.

Material has been drawn from various sources, and in particular the local newspapers, the *Beverley Guardian,* the *Beverley Recorder* and the *Hull Advertiser.* Their use has, we hope, enlivened the text. We have however made every effort to check material drawn from those newspapers against other sources. Many people have helped with information and advice but particular acknowledgement must be made to Keith Allison, the late Philip Brown, Peter Crowther, John Markham, David Neave, and Margaret Noble. We are grateful to David Foster of Humberside Polytechnic for allowing us to use his figures from the 1851 census. We should also like to thank the staffs of Beverley Local History Library, the Humberside County Archives Office, and the University of Hull Photographic Department for their friendly and professional service, and Wendy Munday of Humberside Polytechnic for drawing the maps. Thanks are due to the following for allowing us to reproduce their material: East Yorkshire Borough of Beverley Borough Council for figures 4, 5, 14, 15, 22, 23, 26, 28, 31, 37, 38 and 40, Humberside Arts and Leisure for figures 8, 18, 24, 25, 27 and 35, the Humberside County Archives Office for figure 32, Beverley Race Committee for figure 36, Stuart Witty for figures 10, 11, and 33, Roy Wilson for figure 39, and Gloucester Prison for figure 21.

The text has been written by Jan Crowther, with the assistance of class members:

Anne Fisher
George Higginson
Barbara Needham
Jim Needham
Ann Robinson
Marjorie Salkeld

LIST OF ILLUSTRATIONS

Frontispiece: Beverley Minster from the railway station. (J. J. Sheahan. *Green's ... hand-book to Beverley*, c.1875)

Figure

LIST OF TABLES

Table

INTRODUCTION

A visitor to Beverley, East Yorkshire, in the middle of the 19th century, would have seen a modest market town, unpretentious, but with many attractive pantiled, red-brick houses and cottages. In the 18th century some members of East Riding gentry families had built themselves substantial houses, and the town had developed a flourishing social life, with assemblies, races, a theatre, and other amusements. In the 19th century it retained many of its attractions for the middle classes, and the population included attorneys, physicians, apothecaries, and retired army and navy officers, but it was perhaps less frequented by the upper classes. The town's population in 1851 was 8,915, rising to 10,218 in 1871. Communications were good, since it was situated quite close to the River Hull, to which it was linked by the Beck, a stream canalised in the medieval period, and still of importance for the transportation of produce in the 19th century. A network of turnpiked roads radiated from the town, and the railway linked it to Bridlington to the north, Hull to the south, and, from 1865, York to the west (fig.1)

Beverley was fortunate in possessing extensive common pastures, most notably the Westwood, which bounded the town on the west, and gave the residents an extensive area for recreation, as well as providing pasture for the freemen's animals. On the east of the town lay Figham and Swinemoor, also providing pasture land. The town could present an attractive face to the visitor: Walter White the travel writer came in 1859, and wrote an account of his visit. He described Beverley as having 'a staid, respectable aspect, as if aware of its claims to consideration'. White climbed the Minster tower and wrote:

> *Few towns will bear inspection from above as well as Beverley. It is well built, and is as clean in the rear of the houses as the streets. Looking from such a height, the yards and gardens appear diminished, and the trim flower beds, and leafy arbours, and pebbled paths, and angular plots, and a prevailing neatness, reveal much in favour of the domestic virtues of the inhabitants. And the effect is heightened by the green spaces among the bright red roofs, and the woods which straggle in patches into the town, whereby it retains somewhat of the sylvan aspect for which it was in former times especially remarkable.*

White's comment about the gardens is borne out by contemporary maps. Beverley's larger houses often had extensive grounds, with shrubs, flower beds and kitchen gardens. There were several nurseries where people could perambulate on a sunny day (somewhat reminiscent of the family visit to the garden centre today). Trees were everywhere, and Westwood, Swinemoor and Figham were within easy reach.

The administrative centre of Beverley was the Guildhall in Register Square, where the corporation business was transacted. Councillors were drawn from the ranks of minor industrialists, traders, and the professional classes. Beverley had two Members of Parliament in mid-century, but was disenfranchised in 1870 after the exposure at a public enquiry of the bribery and corruption which had been for years a common feature of its parliamentary and municipal elections. Bribery and treating were all-pervasive, and the town tended to be run by small cliques.

Superficially the town presented a pleasant spectacle to the eye, but underfoot the streets were often badly paved, muddy, or even filthy with householders' refuse. Anthony Trollope certainly did not like Beverley in 1868, when he spent 'in that uninteresting town', 'the most wretched fortnight' of his adult life, canvassing in the election as a Liberal candidate, 'up to [his] knees in slush'. The corporation was very loth to spend money and any decision to improve the surfaces of roads and pavements was preceded by hours of debate. In the small back streets and alleyways of Beverley matters were particularly bad. Several public health reports were produced in the middle of the 19th century, and they gave a very dismal picture of the lives of some inhabitants, crowded into tiny cottages, with little or no drainage or water supply.

Beverley had a small but thriving industrial sector. Tanning had been an important industry since medieval times, and in the 19th century there were several large tanneries, including Hodgson's, on the east side of the town. The coming of the railway encouraged the development of light engineering, and the largest employer in the 1850s was William Crosskill, maker of agricultural machinery, whose works were located close to the station. Near the River Hull at Grovehill was Pennock Tigar's colour manufactory, which switched to the manufacture of fertilisers in 1851. Corn milling on a large scale was conducted by Josiah Crathorne, but there were also many smaller milling businesses. Ship-building was carried out on the River Hull at Grovehill and at Beckside with the vessels being launched sideways because of the narrowness of the river.

The names of Saturday Market Place and Wednesday Market Place commemorate their trading role, but by the 19th century only the former was used for markets. On Saturdays it was packed with stalls and country carriers' carts. Every village within 20 miles sent at least one carrier to Beverley on Saturdays, when the numerous inns and beerhouses did a good trade. There was a fortnightly cattle market in the 19th century, held until 1865 in Norwood, where it broadens out near the junction with Walkergate. In 1865 a new cattle market was opened on its present site between Norwood and Mill Lane. Beverley's quarterly fairs attracted traders from a distance, and a wide range of shops catered for residents and visitors.

The visitors on market days and at the annual hirings sometimes became rowdy, and on occasion had to be brought to law. Beverley in the 19th century was an important centre of justice and poor relief. The county magistrates met at the Sessions House, New Walk, and the borough magistrates met at the Guildhall. At the rear of the Sessions House was the House of Correction, equipped with a treadmill to provide hard labour. Beverley was quite prosperous, but still had its share of poverty. It was the centre of a Poor Law Union, and the union workhouse was in Minster Moorgate until 1861, when a new workhouse was erected on a site overlooking Westwood.

The mid-19th century was a time when religion in Britain was generally flourishing. The Minster was an ornament to the town and drew many visitors, but was rather cold and uncomfortable as a place of worship, whilst St. Mary's seems to have been somewhat dilapidated in mid-century. In Beverley the growth of nonconformity had resulted in the establishment of many chapels, with the Wesleyan and Primitive Methodists particularly well-supported. In 1840 the Anglicans responded by establishing a new place of worship, St. John's Chapel of Ease, in Lairgate. Unlike the Minster it was warm and comfortable, and soon became a favourite resort of the fashionable.

Educational establishments in Beverley were varied. There were a few charity schools where children were educated free, but at most schools fees were charged. The Grammar School, established in the medieval period, and once of high reputation, was in decline in the 1850s and 1860s, and had only a few boarders. The majority of the schools were run by the religious denominations, but there were also many small private schools, those for girls tending to teach 'accomplishments' such as dancing, needlework, and French conversation, rather than academic subjects.

Beverley had a varied social life in mid-Victorian times. The Assembly Rooms, built in the 18th century and enlarged in 1840, provided suitable facilities for travelling players, panoramas, concerts, shows, society dinners, and balls. The races drew people from far afield. Circuses visited the fields and yards at the back of inns. Several societies with modest intellectual aims were established in the middle of the 19th century. The Mechanics' Institute organised talks and debates, and the churches and chapels also ran clubs and societies providing social and educational opportunities. There were commercial circulating libraries, and several reading rooms, where it was possible to read national and local newspapers. The inns and public houses were challenged by a growing temperance movement, which provided concerts, talks, and entertainments for those who wished to avoid strong drink.

In common with most small towns in the mid-Victorian period, Beverley grew in size, and probably in prosperity between 1850 and 1870. Improved trade and communications, better educational opportunities, a wider awareness of the need for cleanliness and public services, and stronger links to the outside world, gradually improved the daily life of most of its inhabitants. The following account of that life reveals a world which, despite many differences, yet has some surprising similarities to life in the town today.

Jan Crowther,
Cottingham 1990.

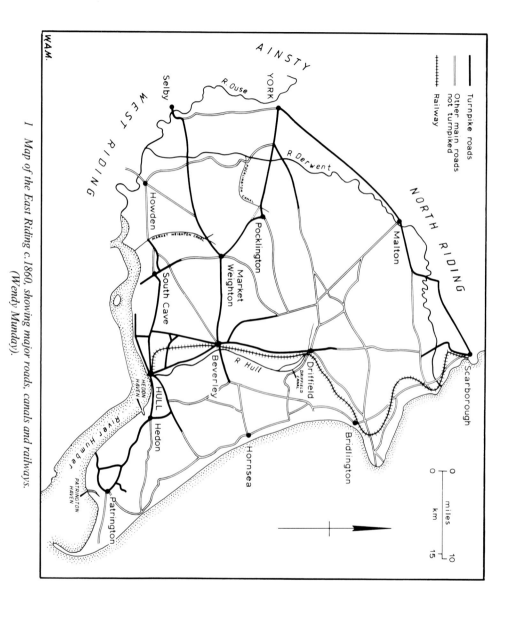

1　Map of the East Riding c.1860, showing major roads, canals and railways.
(Wendy Munday).

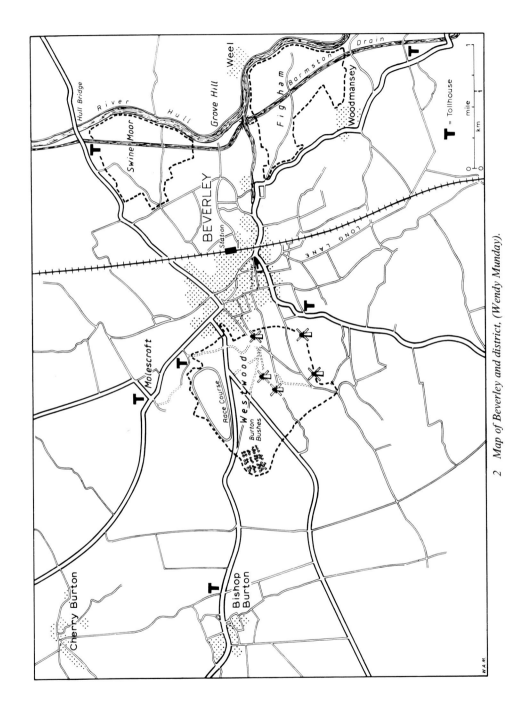

2   *Map of Beverley and district, (Wendy Munday).*

13

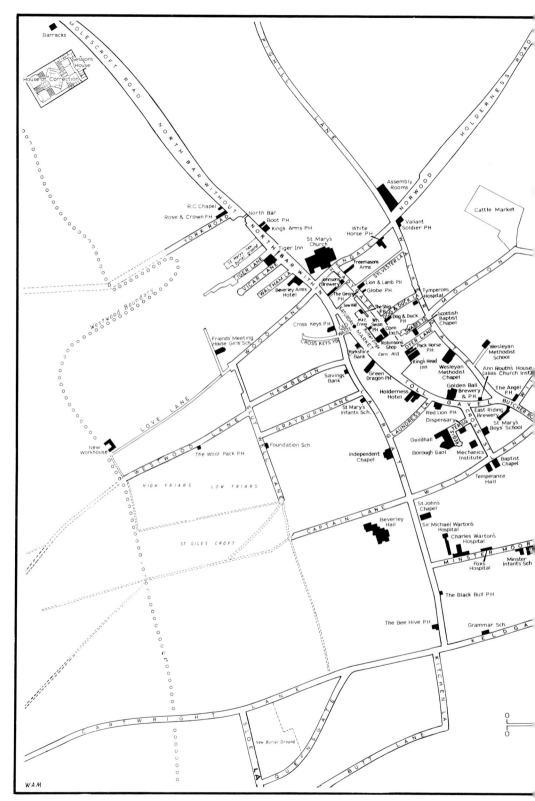

Barracks

MOLESCROFT ROAD

Sessions House

House of Correction

NORTH BAR WITHOUT

DIG HILL LANE

HOLDERNESS ROAD

NORWOOD

Cattle Market

Assembly Rooms

R.C.Chapel
Rose & Crown P.H.
North Bar
Boot P.H.
King's Arms P.H.

YORK ROAD

NORTH BAR WITHIN

WALTHAM LA.

VICAR LANE

TIGER LANE

St Mary's new burial ground

Tiger Inn

St Mary's Church

White Horse P.H.

Valiant Soldier P.H.

Freemasons Arms

Johnson's Brewery

Lion & Lamb P.H.

Beverley Arms Hotel

The George P.H.

Globe P.H.

Tymperons Hospital

Westwood Boundary

HENGATE

SYLVESTER LA.

NORTON

Sow Hill

The Ship P.H.

Dog & Duck P.H.

DOG & DUCK LA.

Scottish Baptist Chapel

Cross Keys P.H.

Friends' Meeting House Girls' Sch.

CROSS KEYS YD.

WOOD LANE

SATURDAY MKT.

Mkt. Cross

Wh. Swan

OLD WASTE

Corn Exch.

SWABY'S YD.

Robinsons Shop

Corn Hill

Pack Horse P.H.

OYER LANE

Wesleyan Methodist School

Yorkshire Bank

NEWBEGIN

Savings Bank

Green Dragon P.H.

King's Head Inn

Wesleyan Methodist Chapel

Ann Routh's House (alias Church Inst.)

LOVE LANE

SCOTT LANE

GRAYBURN LANE

St Mary's Infants Sch.

Holderness Hotel

Golden Ball Brewery & P.H.

East Riding Brewery

The Angel P.H.

BUTCHER RO

New Workhouse

The Wool Pack P.H.

WESTWOOD ROAD

WELL LANE

Foundation Sch.

Red Lion P.H.

Dispensary

St Mary's Boys' School

Independent Chapel

Guildhall

Borough Gaol

Mechanics Institute

Baptist Chapel

Temperance Hall

HIGH FRIARS

LOW FRIARS

CAPTAIN LANE

ST GILES CROFT

Beverley Hall

St.Johns Chapel

Sir Michael Warton's Hospital

Charles Warton's Hospital

MINSTER MOOR

Foxs Hospital

Minster Infants Sch

The Black Bull P.H.

The Bee Hive P.H.

Grammar Sch.

KELDGA

KITCHEN LA.

CARTWRIGHT ROAD

SLOP LANE

QUEENSGATE

New Burial Ground

BUTT LANE

WAM

14

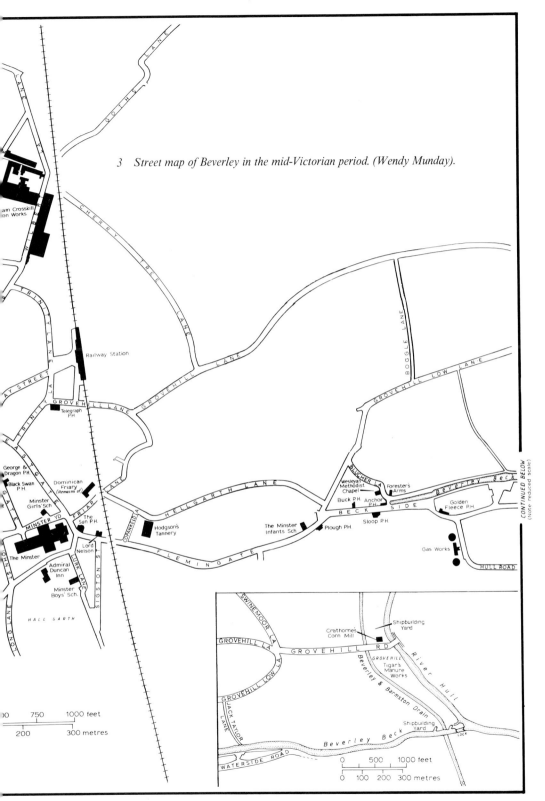

3   Street map of Beverley in the mid-Victorian period. (Wendy Munday).

15

CHAPTER ONE
TOWN MANAGEMENT

Beverley's corporation had been reformed in 1835 under the Municipal Corporations Act. The new council consisted of 18 councillors, six aldermen and a mayor. Councillors served for three years for one of two wards, St. Mary's and the Minster. They were elected by all adult male rate-payers. Aldermen were elected by the councillors, and served for six years, three standing down every three years. The mayor held office for one year, but was often re-elected. One important result of the new system was a change in the socio-economic background of the council. In the early 19th century the mayor and the majority of the aldermen, had come from the gentry or professional classes. After 1835 tradesmen and manufacturers, such as William Brigham, grocer, and William Crosskill, machine-maker, took office as mayors. Many of them were Liberals, and party politics began to play a more important part than hitherto in the administration of the town.

The Beverley and East Riding Reform Association was founded in 1835 by the Liberals, to be followed a few years later by the Beverley Conservative Association. Both were to be highly influential in municipal and parliamentary politics. Bribery and corruption were widespread in the political life of the town and were practised on such a scale that Beverley was to become a byword nationally for such practices. They flourished principally on account of the willingness shown by the parliamentary candidates to spend large sums of money to purchase votes in order to secure their election to Parliament. However bribery was not confined to parliamentary elections since prospective candidates made use of the local elections in order to build up their power base. Eventually the situation became so scandalous that in 1869 a Royal Commission was set up to investigate bribery at Beverley elections since the early 1850s. The evidence that emerged was of no surprise to Beverlonians, who, according to one witness had 'drunk in the system with their mother's milk', but it created considerable interest nationally, the *Times* carrying daily reports from the hearing, and devoting several editorials to the subject. As a result of their findings the Commissioners recommended the disenfranchisement of the borough.

Beverley had sent two M.P.s to Westminster. A parliamentary election was a popular event in Beverley, since if it were to be hotly contested 'the conduits were so full [with bribery money] they never ran'. The Commissioners estimated that out of a constituency of 1,100 (before the extension of the franchise in 1867) about 800 were open to bribery, comprising 300 who had no 'political principles or likings, ... locally known as 'rolling stock'' and about 250 others on either side who, if they knew that money was being paid out, would not vote unless they were bribed. Voters were paid both in money and in vouchers which could be exchanged for drink or provisions. The arrangements for paying out bribes varied from one election to another, as did the sums

17

offered, which could go as high as £3 per voter, the equivalent of about three weeks' wages for an ordinary working man. In 1857 the Conservatives bribed quite openly in the Market Place. An agent told the Commission 'I asked them what they would take and bought them as cheap as I could'. In 1859 the Liberals paid out sovereigns to their voters in a building which had one of its entrances in Toll Gavel and the other in Walkergate. The voters walked through a passage in semi-darkness, passing what appeared in the half-light to be a pump, but which turned out to be a man who placed money in their hands. After that election there was a petition to Parliament alleging bribery on the part of both successful candidates. As a result Walters, the Liberal, was deprived of his seat. The consequent bye-election of 1860 was more discreetly managed, with a stranger 'in a hairy cap' distributing the money on behalf of the Liberals. The Conservatives, who also bribed on a large scale, won the seat. At the 1865 election the Liberals used the Mechanics' Institute Hall as a venue for passing bribes. The method was described in the Commission's Report thus:

> *An aperture was made in the folding doors of the library ... just large enough to permit a man's hand to be thrust through it; behind this door stood or sat the briber, with a bag of gold before him; the voters were directed to pass through the room, the number being called out, a sovereign or two as the case might be, was pushed through the aperture ...*

Nevertheless the Conservative candidates won the seats because of their party's patient groundwork in gaining control over the institutions of the town. At Beverley's last election in 1868 it was estimated that 1,000 persons out of a total electorate of 2,762 had received payment for their votes. It was at that election that Anthony Trollope, the novelist, stood as one of the Liberal candidates. Neither he nor his colleague had bribed, and they came bottom of the poll. Trollope was disgusted by what he saw in Beverley, and impatient with the 'bores and fools' encountered there. He used it as a model for the town with a corrupt electorate in his novel *Ralph the heir*.

The electoral process itself was conducive to bribery, not only in Beverley but in many other towns where until the introduction of a secret ballot in 1872 corruption and intimidation were widely practised. The formal proceedings for an election began with the erection of the hustings in Saturday Market Place. The supporters of each party assembled in force, displaying their colours, crimson for the Conservatives (blue in most other towns), and orange for the Liberals. The candidates arrived in procession on horseback. In 1857 the *Beverley Guardian* described the scene inaugurating an election. 'Well-dressed ladies with coloured flowers in their hair' sat on the platform. The mayor was received with 'cheers, groans hisses', and questions such as 'What about the lower classes?'. After the candidates had been proposed there were lengthy speeches, constantly interrupted. Polling began the next day at 8 a.m. The poll was conducted openly and a poll book was published later so that party agents could check that the people who had been paid had voted correctly. Alcohol flowed freely at election time, voters either being bribed with the offer of drink or induced to drink by the opposition in the hope that they might be too inebriated to arrive at the polling booth.

After the declaration the winning candidates together with their supporters went in procession through the town. In the 1857 bye-election Sir Henry Edwards, the victorious Conservative candidate, was preceded by a game cock and a stuffed fox 'adorned with crimson feathers'. Beverlonians might not see their members of parliament again until the next election but the members' representatives in the town ensured that their interests were maintained. The same people who managed the parliamentary elections were also involved in the conduct of municipal elections. That had always been the case, but from mid-century the parties became better organised. It emerged at the Bribery Commission Inquiry that especially after the arrival in Beverley of Sir Henry Edwards as a Conservative candidate in 1857 that party built up an almost unassailable hold over the institutions of the town, beginning with the corporation, but including the pasture masters, the administration of certain charities, and even the election of St. Mary's church wardens. Edwards even bought William Crosskill's foundry in 1864, ostensibly as an act of charity, but in reality to create yet another base for patronage. The manager of the foundry, who was a placeman brought from outside the town by Edwards, the secretary and the foremen of the various departments, as well as most of the employees, were either recipients or dispensers of bribery money.

Party allegiance became increasingly important in the council chamber throughout the mid-Victorian period. Bribery money which had tended to be distributed mainly at polling time, began to come in steadily between elections, principally on the Conservative side with the consequent shift in the balance of power in that party's favour. Because the council employed large numbers of tradesmen and craftsmen it was in a position to give or withhold employment according to political allegiance. Council meetings, which were conducted in the Guildhall in Register Square (fig. 4), were lively and informal affairs with insults swapped as a matter of course. Matters became more acrimonious from the late 1850s as the Conservatives gained the upper hand. At that time there were two Beverley newspapers to fan the flames of party rivalry, the Conservative *Guardian*, and the Liberal *Recorder*.

The leading lights in the Liberal party in the mid-Victorian period included Daniel Boyes, the landlord of the Angel and so-called 'Prime Minister' of Beverley, the industrialists William Crosskill, Richard Hodgson and (until his death in 1851) Pennock Tigar, Dr. Sandwith, and Joseph Hind. Prominent Conservatives included the solicitors, Thomas Champney and H. E. Sylvester, doctors John Arden and Charles Brereton, and the draper William Wreghitt, who was soon to become notorious as the unofficial Conservative agent, and co-ordinator of the campaign to take control of the borough.

After the election of Sir Henry Edwards in 1857, Wreghitt, backed by large sums of money from Edwards, began to work towards the replacement by Conservatives of all the Liberals on the council. The Commission Report found that:

> it became a settled plan of action between Edwards, Wreghitt, and the candidates for the town council, that at every municipal

contest Wreghitt should supply the funds that might be deemed necessary to secure their return; and accordingly the practice of purchasing votes at these elections became general and systematic ... From 1859 to 1869 the supporters ... of Sir Henry Edwards obtained and exercised an almost absolute control in the public and municipal affairs of Beverley.

Not content with that Wreghitt also brought the pasture masters under his control. Prior to 1835 the pastures had been administered by the corporation, but after that date their management was vested in 12 pasture masters elected annually by the freemen. In the 1840s and 1850s election to the office of pasture master was not a party matter, but Wreghitt soon made it so, and after 1860 all the pasture masters were Conservatives. The powers of patronage of the pasture masters were quite considerable, especially because they managed Walker's Pasture Freemen's Gift, a charity established for deserving freemen who had had lost animals or who were in distress. It was revealed by the Inquiry that from 1860 until 1869 Conservatives benefited from Walker's Gift to an inordinate degree. One man bought a sick horse by arrangement for £3. When it died the following day, he received £1 10s for the carcase, followed by £3 from the pasture masters for his misfortune, and had £1 10s returned, as previously arranged, from the vendor. Other cases of abuse also came to light at the Inquiry.

Another method of obtaining influence which Wreghitt used was the financing of apprentices who were in a position to become freemen of the town. Having finished their apprenticeship they could become freemen on payment of £2 10s. For the promise of their support for the Conservative cause Wreghitt was prepared to pay their entry fee. At a much lower price than that needed for a borough election, he also managed to ensure that the churchwardens of St. Mary's church were Conservative supporters, since they too had plenty of work to offer tradesmen owing to the church's considerable property in the town. Between 1859 and 1869 Edwards and his Conservative running mates paid out enormous sums of money to voters in Beverley. The Commission was unable to ascertain exactly how much, because all the papers had been destroyed by those concerned as soon as they had realised that there was to be an inquiry. But Sir James Walker, whose son was M.P. from 1860 until 1865, admitted to having paid out £5,200 over that period, and Christopher Sykes, who followed Walker in 1865, paid out a similar sum. Edwards himself must have expended thousands of pounds to retain the honour of representing Beverley at Westminster.

All this was revealed at the Inquiry. The Commission sat in Beverley for six weeks, and the printed minutes of evidence fill over 700 pages. Beverlonians faced each other in the witness box, contradicting each other and retracting their evidence when it became apparent that they had lied or dissembled. The antagonisms which were engendered by the Inquiry must have taken a generation or more to dissipate. After 1870, when the Commissioners made their recommendations, and Beverley lost its M.P.s, the town had to establish a new equilibrium.

4   *Guildhall, Register Square. Luke Clennell, c.1835. (East Yorkshire Borough of Beverley Borough Council).*

5   *Saturday Market Place. J. Barrie Robinson, c.1850. (East Yorkshire Borough of Beverley Borough Council).*

The council, corrupt as it may have been, still had certain responsibilities, though by modern standards they were relatively light. It managed the Beck and the Grammar School, administered the police, repaired the streets, and controlled the corporation property. From 1851, as a result of the application to the town of the 1848 Public Health Act, the council constituted itself a local board of health, which meant that it took over (from the Improvement Commission which dated from 1808), the overseeing of street lighting, gas supply, and cleansing, and that it was obliged under the Act to appoint an Inspector of Nuisances, who could report any problems which would pose a danger to public health. The income of the council came from tolls taken on the Beck, tolls from markets and fairs, property rents, investments, and the collection of a modest watch rate and pump rate. Those added together brought in about £2,000 per annum.

In the 1850s and 1860s there were usually five or six separate committees set up by the council from its own members: the Beck Committee, the Paving and Flagging Committee, the Watch Committee, the Gas Committee, the Property Committee, and the Finance Committee. They reported to the council regularly, during its monthly meetings. The Beck Committee was responsible for keeping the waterway clear, for maintaining equipment such as cranes, for ensuring that the lock-keeper performed his duties satisfactorily, and for collecting tolls paid by vessels using the Beck. Revenue from Beck tolls could be quite substantial: in 1848-9 £615 was obtained, and in the second half of the century earnings often exceeded £700. Some of that money was used to repair the town's roads and footways, responsibility for which was vested in the Beck Committee at those times when a committee for paving and flagging had not been appointed.

From 1824 the streets were lit with gas. The gas works, the gateway of which still stands, was at first a private undertaking, but in 1828 the corporation bought it and thereafter became responsible for the manufacture of gas, as well as for the illumination of the town. Some lamps were placed upon walls, but many were on iron posts, which bore the name of John Malam, who established the gas-works, or of William Crosskill, the iron-founder. Several Malam and Crosskill lamp-posts are still in use, now lit by electricity. The lamps were lit at dusk and extinguished at 11 p.m. by nightwatchmen-cum-constables. There was a steady increase in the number of lamps, as there was of the demand for gas from private individuals. At first only public buildings were gas-lit, but gradually more and more people began to use gas for lighting. In 1855 the manager of the gas works wrote that 'gas will soon be required generally for cooking as well as lighting', and several of the ironmongers began stocking gas cookers. In 1859 the receipts from private gas consumers were £1,731 15s 8d. Some of the larger gas lamps were quite imposing and ornamental: one in the centre of Saturday Market Place was protected with iron railings, which were only removed in 1860.

There is plenty of evidence from contemporary reports that the repair of the streets was not carried out to the satisfaction of most townspeople. Badly paved streets could be a health hazard in themselves, but when they were combined with inadequate drainage and an ignorance of the causes of disease matters could reach a serious state. In 1849, empowered by the Public Health Act of 1848, and concerned lest the cholera epidemic which was raging in Hull should arrive in Beverley, a number of townspeople petitioned for the Act to be applied to the town. An inspector, G. T. Clark, was sent to report on the sanitary state of Beverley. He found that the town was a 'remarkable instance of a place which has reached a very high rate of mortality, while a large portion of the inhabitants have believed it to be particularly healthy'. His report revealed that behind the principal streets, which presented a reasonably attractive facade, there lurked overcrowded foetid yards with overflowing privies and cesspits, blocked gutters, and broken pavements. Clark also commented upon the reluctance of the townspeople to spend money upon improvements to the town.

The streets were paved with cobble stones, which were brought to the town by sea from Spurn Head, or by land from Hornsea beach. The surfaces of the streets were often full of holes, and needed constant attention, which they did not always receive. A report in September 1857 noted that in Saturday Market Place gravel and cobbles lay about near the election hustings, and almost caused the upset of a horse and gig one night. Another hazard, after the introduction of gas to the town, was the uneven road surfaces caused by lack of care in re-laying the pavements or cobbles after the digging of trenches for gas mains. Since the demand for gas kept rising in the first half of the 19th century new pipes were constantly being put in. The laying of gas pipes under the streets was the first of many utilities which required holes in the road —water, sewage, electricity and telephones were yet to come.

In February 1858 a new gas main was to be laid in Saturday Market Place. Daniel Boyes said it would be an excellent opportunity to have the Market Place properly drained and levelled, and thus 'to do away with the gutter or rather river, which often exists in the centre of it, much to the annoyance of carriers and others attending the market'. The council agreed to start the work in the summer, disrupting not only the Midsummer Fair but also the weekly markets. In August there was a memorial to the council from the principal tradesmen requesting that carriers' carts should be restored to their former position in the Market Place, which was apparently full of piles of soil. Cattle, 'which were a source of annoyance to females and others passing along North Bar Street', should also be returned to the Market Place. Councillor Fox hoped 'that the carriers would soon go back again. They were a curious lot of folks and he had been told ... that if they were not removed they would go to Driffield'. In September the soil was still there. It was reported that vehicles could hardly pass, and stallholders were standing up to their ankles in water in wet weather (fig. 5).

Holes, pools of water, and animals were not the only hazards. Unnecessary 'road furniture' could cause considerable inconvenience, even danger, as exemplified by a letter to the *Beverley Guardian* in February 1858 complaining of:

> *two ugly posts, which are stuck in the centre of each end of the footways through the North Bar, and for what earthly purpose I fancy only God knows, ... and in addition to the danger and*

inconvenience ... they serve for a lot of idle fellows to lounge upon and merely cause them to congregate and insult with revolting and indecent language whoever may be passing.

The pavements of the principal streets were flagged, and were themselves kept quite clean, but the open gutters were irregular, and full of refuse. The lanes, courts, and alleys between and beyond the principal streets were much worse. Many of the yards were unpaved, a serious health hazard, since rubbish and refuse was thrown down upon their surfaces. With only limited money at its disposal the council often had to decide whether to repair and maintain streets already paved, or to extend paving to more minor streets. People who lived in areas which were not paved at all, for example Keldgate and Minster Moorgate, were very unhappy when their streets were ignored at the expense of more central parts of the town. In 1856 it was estimated that it would cost £157 3s 7d to renew the road surface of Norwood. That included preparation, flagging, curbstones, and small paving cobbles. In 1865 a letter was sent to the *Beverley Guardian* purporting to come from Well Lane, a small street off Butcher Row, complaining that 'its neighbours have received great improvement, but it has been neglected, having no member of the corporation resident on its borders'.

Clark's report, and subsequent reports from the council subcommittee findings reveal the considerable inadequacies of Beverley's 'public services' in the 1850s and 1860s. Many of the problems stemmed paradoxically from the favourable position of the town, which was intersected by water courses which over the centuries had been used as open sewers. By the 19th century they had become totally inadequate to deal with the quantity of waste matter being poured into them. The principal sewer ran from Bar Dyke, just outside the North Bar, and into Walker Beck, which ran across Minster Moorgate, Keldgate, and Long Lane, emptying into the water mill dam. The dam naturally caused a serious obstruction in the flow, and consequently there was often a build-up of sewage. Throughout its course this sewer received soiled water, rubbish of every description, and even the contents of privies. In places it had been arched over by the owners of adjacent property, so that its width, height, and state of repair were subject to considerable variation. Houses had even been built on top of it, some of them with their floors only inches above the noisome contents. A second major sewer began in Highgate, ran down Hell Garth Lane near Flemingate, and emptied into the Beck. Its proximity to the tanneries meant that it received their waste matter. The solid contents were retained in two tanks at the head of the Beck, whilst the liquids passed into the river, though the lock, which had been built in the early part of the century, slowed down the flow. Another large sewer, which ran along Wilbert Lane, and crossed Grovehill Lane, also emptied into the Beck. Many smaller open sewers ran into the larger ones.

The open drains in the small yards which occupied the space between the larger streets were often choked up with refuse, and Clark found many places where foul water could only run away into the street. In some yards there was no drainage whatever. In Flemingate were several courts called Taylor's Rows, where the houses had no back openings, the floors were below the surface of the ground, and privies had been built against the walls. The yards were unpaved and undrained, and manure, ashes, and household refuse lay in heaps, and many residents kept pigs. Some of the worst cases concerned new houses, which had been built for the poorer classes by jerry-builders making a quick profit. Clark wrote:

In Tiger Lane is a row of new houses. In the confined space at the back and close to the doors are the privies and middens which must, when the manure is suffered to accumulate, ... be very offensive. This place is at present neither paved nor drained.

Clark admitted that people living in yards with no drainage 'had of necessity [to throw] the slops and filth from culinary operations' onto the ground. Their sanitary arrangements were, as might be expected, equally rudimentary. But so were those of most Beverlonians at that time. Clark said that:

most, even of the cottages, have privies, but these, except in a few cases where they are placed over the public ditch, are built by the side of an open cesspool, which is the common receptacle for the ashes and ordinary household refuse.

Not all houses had their own privies. Clark noted many cases of one privy to four or more houses or cottages. Some householders had a privy to themselves but had to travel some distance to get to it. In Burgess Yard, Lairgate, at the back of the present Cross Keys were several privies which were let to:

persons residing in the very respectable shops and houses in Lairgate fronting into Market place which are said to have no privies whatever. It is however far better that these inferior and distant conveniences should be adopted rather than cesspools should be sunk beneath the houses which would be the only other alternative in the present state of the drainage of the town.

The contents of cesspits were bought by farmers to put on their land. Clark recorded that five shillings per house was paid. Removal through yards, or worse, through houses could cause considerable difficulty. In Ladygate where 'the houses are built back to back, or nearly so, in solid blocks, the night soil is removed in boxes, and in practice, appears to be thrown out into the private lanes'. At that time there was a depot for night soil and ashes between Railway Street and Trinity Lane, 'much complained of as injuring the adjacent property', which speculators were hoping to sell to the professional classes.

There was no shortage of water in Beverley, situated as it was upon a spring line. The corporation was responsible for 33 public pumps in the 1850s, and levied a small pump rate for their maintenance. There were also several hundred private pumps in the town. In general the water seems to have been good, but Clark found polluted wells in some yards, where middens and cesspits were situated too close to the water supply. He suggested that a piped water supply using water pumped by steam from the River Hull should be introduced, since all those improvements in drainage and sanitation which he

6   *New Walk and Sessions House. (J. J. Sheahan.* **Green's ... hand-book to Beverley,** *c.1875).*

7   *Former dispensary, Register Square. (P. A. Crowther).*

advocated needed a constant supply of water. Whether his scheme would have been practical or not was never put to the test. The corporation decided that Beverley's present system was perfectly adequate. Later attempts to introduce a water works also failed, and it was not until the 1880s that one was built.

Very few of Clark's other recommendations were taken up by the corporation, owing to their reluctance to increase the rates to raise the necessary money. They probably gauged the attitude of their voters correctly in making that decision. The application of the Public Health Act to the town did result in some minor improvements. An Inspector of Nuisances was appointed, and his tasks included inspecting lodging houses to ensure that they were not overcrowded and that the accommodation was clean, overseeing the cleaning of streets, and reporting on the state of drains and sewers. He also acted upon complaints about nuisances such as slaughter houses, tripe-boiling, and manure heaps. New houses had to be provided with proper privies, cesspools, and drains, and when builders wanted to build new streets the plans had to be submitted to the board of health.

Overcrowded burial grounds could be a serious health hazard, and those in Beverley were 'very crowded indeed' according to Clark. In 1851 there were three principal grave-yards: the Minster yard, St. Mary's yard, and a burial ground opened in 1829 just inside North Bar which also belonged to St. Mary's. In the Minster yard there were over 150 burials annually and it was so full that corpses had to be buried only three feet below ground. St. Mary's yard was even more overcrowded. The new burial ground, which had not been much used in the 1830s and 1840s, because people felt that burials should take place in the immediate vicinity of the church, was being used more frequently by the 1850s. The churchwardens of St. Mary's stated that 276 persons had been buried there by 1851, and estimated that there was room for a further 3,724. They based their calculations upon the size of the area (2,000 square yards), the fact that 'one half of the number of funerals are of children under 14', and their allowance of 21 square feet for an adult's grave and six square feet for a child's.

In 1859 St. Mary's churchyard was closed except for interment in family vaults, and no more burials were allowed in the Wesleyan Chapel or the Independent Chapel burial grounds. A meeting was held in the same year about the advisability of having a cemetery for the whole town. During a discussion on the best location Daniel Boyes suggested the Westwood. A cemetery company was formed, but subsequently wound up when the parishes could not agree on the arrangements. Two separate grounds were acquired in 1860 for the parishes of St. Martin's and St. John's which were both served by the Minster. St. Martin's burial ground was in Cartwright Lane, and St. John's in Queensgate. The Minster churchyard was closed for burials, except in existing plots, in 1861. In 1864 land on Molescroft Road was offered as a burial ground for the parishioners of St. Mary's by Rachel Myers, who, three years later, became the first person to be interred there. Apparently burials were still taking place at that time in family plots in St. Mary's churchyard, for the *Beverley Guardian* reported that grave-digging was resulting in coffins being cut in two, and piles of bones having to be re-buried indiscriminately.

In the 19th century fire-fighting was undertaken by a combination of parish, corporation, and private initiative. Each parish had an engine and the council contributed a yearly sum to their upkeep. In 1831 an engine had also been bought from subscriptions raised in the town. The engines were kept in the Minster and St. Mary's, though from 1841 those under the care of the churchwardens of St. Mary's were kept in a near-by house. A report of 1854 stated that those engines were in good repair, but that the two at the Minster were derelict. When a fire broke out it was usual to alert the town by ringing the church bells. In May 1858 a fire started at 2 a.m. in Johnson's brewery, Ladygate, and the fire bells of the Minster and St. Mary's were sounded. St. Mary's fire engine was brought out, and, having recently undergone extensive repairs it performed efficiently. It was placed in Sylvester Lane, opposite the brewery, and was able to draw plentiful supplies of water from pumps in the Market Place and the brewery itself. People appeared to fight the fire armed with buckets, and it was subdued in one and a half hours.

It was recognised by the owners of various industrial enterprises that total dependence upon the borough fire engines was inadvisable. Therefore when a Fire Engines Committee was appointed by the corporation to investigate the state of the fire engines in 1861, it was able to report that there were two extra engines, one belonging to Crosskill's ironworks, and one kept at Grovehill, presumably provided by Tigar's manure works and the ship-builders. The Committee suggested that a fire brigade should be established, consisting of a superintendent, a deputy, 'two tube men, two pipe men, two watermen, two suction men, and two roofers'. The brigade should be drawn from suitable trades, preferably masons, joiners, bricklayers, plasterers, sweeps, mechanics, and saddlers, and be aged 30 to 45 years. The superintendent should be paid £4 per annum for looking after the engines, and his deputy £2 for keeping them clean. When the brigade was called out to a fire they should be paid 2s 6d for the first hour and 1s 6d for every subsequent hour, whilst the firemen should get 2s for the first hour and 1s 6d for every subsequent hour. In the event of a false alarm the superintendent and deputy should be paid 1s 6d and the firemen 1s. All firemen were to live close to the engines, and to have a notice 'fireman' over their doors. A hat band with the inscription 'fireman', would be issued to them. The watchmen should know their addresses and be responsible for calling them out.

Whether all those arrangements were carried out in their entirety is unclear from the records. In 1867 there was another discussion on fire-fighting services. By that date the subscription engine was kept at the Guildhall under the supervision of the superintendent of the police. There were four other engines: the large Minster engine which was kept at Crosskill's foundry, a smaller engine kept at the Minster, one belonging to the Iron and Waggon Company, and the Grovehill engine. The superintendent of the police reported that the Guildhall engine needed repair, and if that were done it would be quite capable of throwing water over the top of the Yorkshire Bank in Saturday Market Place. There were about two dozen firemen, 'some of whom were the greatest blackguards and riff-raff of the town, who only came up at the last minute when a fire was out and still expected to be paid'. His criticisms called forth an indignant letter to the *Beverley Guardian* from the superintendent of the fire brigade, asserting the respectability of his men. As a result of the enquiry the subscription engine was mended and its serviceability demonstrated in front of the council in Saturday Market Place, when a sufficient force of water was obtained to go right over the parapet of the Yorkshire Bank, 'as great a height as ever they would require in the town'. The council decided that they should continue to subscribe £3 annually to its support, and that the charge for its service should be £2 10s per fire, or 20s if taken out but not used.

It seems that the councillors only acted when a situation was critical. They were not prepared to undertake any large-scale improvements but spent hours debating minor changes. Considerable attention was paid to the enhancement and preservation of New Walk (fig. 6) as an attractive entrance to the town and a place for perambulation. In the 1780s it had been laid out as a promenade with seats and tastefully planted trees. There was a fine of £5 on anyone who committed acts of vandalism there, which must have helped to protect the area. An avenue of horse chestnut trees was planted in the 1820s, protected by railings. In May 1858, when the railings were to be repaired and painted or else removed, the trees were well grown up, and Daniel Boyes stated that the railings were now useless — 'boys ran along the tops and swung on the gates'.

In 1867, the council, stimulated to action by the prospect of a visit from the Royal Archaeological Society, turned its attention to the state of North Bar, which at that time was covered with plaster and whitewash. William Wreghitt suggested that it should be covered over with a rough coating of cement, which would last for 100 years. Others wanted to return the Bar 'to its original character'. An ironic suggestion that a 'Committee of Taste' should be formed was not adopted. It was decided to chip off the plaster and repair the brickwork.

At election time much was made of the improvements recently carried out. In 1868 they were able to boast of the iron seats that had been placed near the Beck for people to sit and smoke upon. Wooden ones had been rejected because those which had been placed on the road to Molescroft had been defaced 'in an offensive and disgusting manner'. One innovation no doubt much appreciated was the public urinal which was placed in 1863 in a passage near the Corn Exchange. It may well have been Beverley's first public convenience. Certainly there was nothing of that description in the Market Place in 1858, when a resident complained to the *Beverley Guardian* of Old Waste being 'very offensive to occupants and public decency by want of public urinals ... the effects [being] visible inside adjoining houses'.

Poor drainage, polluted water, and inferior housing conditions, meant that Beverley had a death rate of 31.3 per thousand in the late 1840s compared with only 20.5 for the surrounding villages. The medical needs of the population were met by physicians, surgeons, and apothecaries. The upper classes called upon the services of Dr. Sandwith, Dr. Brereton, and Dr. Boulton, whose imposing residences demonstrated that their services were not for those of limited means. Surgeons and apothecaries could supply medicines, advice, and perform minor operations. Beverley had no hospital, but from 1823 there was a dispensary, which was established under the will of William Wilson, and was intended to provide medicine for the sick poor. It was supported throughout its life by subscriptions and donations. Initially it was in Lairgate, but in 1828 a new building was erected in Register Square (fig. 7). The rules show that the dispensary was intended only for the 'really necessitous', which excluded living-in servants (who should be taken care of by their employers), or persons on parish relief (who would receive help from the poor rates).

Persons wishing to use the dispensary had to obtain a recommendation from one of the sponsors, who were provided with forms according to the amount of money they had subscribed. Those who gave one guinea annually were entitled to recommend 30 persons per annum. The medical practitioners of the town gave their services free, and attended in turn, on Tuesdays and Fridays. There was a resident apothecary-cum-dispenser, who was responsible for making up prescriptions and keeping records. Drugs cost about £60 per annum in mid-century. In 1846 an electrifying machine had been donated, but there is no record of its application. In 1854 the annual report stated that of 752 patients treated, 587 were cured, 70 were relieved, 30 died, 42 remained on the books, and 23 were 'irregular'. By 1860 the numbers had risen markedly: of 1,347 people treated, 1,225 were cured, 62 relieved, 24 died, and 36 were still on the books. In 1854 the most common complaint was diarrhoea. In 1860 there were 40 cases of smallpox, but only one was fatal. The report of 1864 included 32 cases of chicken pox, eight of small pox, 112 of measles, 94 of diarrhoea, 32 of dysentry, 42 of scarlatina, 64 of bronchitis and other respiratory diseases, 155 of fever, and 94 of catarrh. Small pox vaccinations were being offered free to the poor at that time. Beverley was very fortunate in avoiding the devastating cholera outbreak which hit Hull in 1849. In August of that year ten paupers died of the disease in Beverley workhouse, but it did not spread further into the town.

CHAPTER TWO
COMMERCE AND INDUSTRY

Beverley had a thriving industrial area, mainly located around the Beck and at Grovehill near the River Hull. The range of its economic activities, retailing, trading, financial, and industrial, was quite extensive, but the town's proximity to Hull limited its economic development, especially after 1846, when the railway from Hull to Bridlington was opened. Market and fair days were well-attended however, and provided opportunities for country people to come into the town both to buy and to sell.

Directories show the number of businesses in the town, and the census reveals how many people were employed in the various sectors. The 1851 census shows that 383, almost ten per cent of the working population of Beverley, were involved in retailing and trading, over half of them being engaged in the food trade. There were 55 people selling clothing and fabrics, but to those could be added a further 328 who were making clothes or involved in textile production. They included 88 tailors, 47 milliners, 169 dressmakers and seamstresses, together with staymakers, straw bonnet makers, hatters, patten makers (a type of clog), and a breeches maker. Beverley then had three general dyers, one silk dyer, seven weavers, a bleacher, three linen blue makers, and one hemp spinner, all that was left of its once-thriving textile industry. There were also 132 shoemakers, and one 'boot closer'.

Tables 1, 2, 3 and 4 show actual businesses, retailing, trading, crafts, manufacturing, services and agricultural, listed in directories for 1851, 1858 and 1867. Some caution is required when making comparisons between directories, which may be subject to error for several reasons: the collection of data varied over time, different headings were sometimes used, and some smaller tradesmen may not have been included. Moreover the separation of retailers and craftsmen in the tables may give a false picture. In the 19th century there was less distinction between retailers, craftsmen and manufacturers: for example many tailors, milliners and boot and shoemakers sold their products directly to the public. Nevertheless the tables do reveal the wide range of businesses operating in Beverley.

The category 'shopkeepers' used in directories probably refers to those general household retailers, the non-specialist 'corner shops', which were usually located in the lower-class residential parts of the town. The high-class shops, such as linen drapers, haberdashers, booksellers and grocers, were usually located in the centre of the town, in or near Saturday Market Place.

The 1851 census shows that there was a high concentration of drapers, haberdashers, and silk mercers, mostly located on the western side of the Market Place. Several ran quite large establishments, employing many assistants, who often lived on the premises, thus enabling the shopkeeper to exercise greater control over his or her staff, and allowing the shop to be manned for the very long hours of business usual in mid-century. Many shops in the summer remained open until nine or ten o'clock at night.

Family businesses were usual. Even in those establishments where a large staff was employed members of the family frequently worked in the shop. Many shops were kept by women, who had often taken over the business on the death of their husbands. In 1851 women trading in the Market Place included Elizabeth Taylor, a gunmaker whose two sons also worked in that trade, Rosabella Newstead, a grocer who employed a manager and four living-in assistants, Sarah Shaw, a draper, who had two living-in apprentices, and two sisters, Sarah and Elizabeth Ranson, haberdashers and Berlin wool dealers. In 1851 one third of all the general shopkeepers listed in the directories were women.

Contemporary illustrations show that the houses and shops in Saturday Market Place were very varied in their architectural styles, and presented an even more attractively diverse aspect than they do at the present day. However, some of the older buildings were being replaced, often by much larger ones. In 1851 window tax was abolished, after having been levied since 1697, and some shopkeepers in Beverley responded by modernising their shop fronts and introducing plate glass windows. But many of an older style remained, and indeed still do. Fig. 8 shows Saturday Market Place in c.1860. On the left the Green Dragon's sign can be seen. To the north of the Green Dragon in 1851 were the premises of John Brigham, grocer and seed merchant. The census records that he employed 18 men, most of them probably at his Beckside warehouse. In 1853 Brigham's shop and the one next door were sold to Charles Hobson, a chemist and druggist, who had an imposing shop built on the site (shown in fig. 8), now occupied partly by Foster's. The owner of the adjoining shop to Brigham's in 1851 was John Green, a printer, bookseller and stationer, who was quite a newcomer in the Market Place, having moved there recently from Hengate. In 1851 he employed two men and two apprentice printers, and had established a circulating library. In 1853 he moved south of the Green Dragon to larger premises, where he started the town's second newspaper, the *Beverley Guardian*, and where the firm remained until the late 1970s.

North of Green's was a tailor and draper, followed by another draper's, managed by a widow, with two apprentices living on the premises, whilst next door to that was the largest establishment in the Market Place, W. G. Drewery's, drapers, milliners, and dressmakers. Drewery employed 21 shop assistants, five of whom lived with him on the premises. On the site now occupied by Briggs and Powell was the premises of John Clark, ironmonger, brazier, and gas-fitter. Clark employed three men, four apprentices, and an errand boy, none of whom lived on the premises. The Yorkshire Bank occupied the same site as the National Westminster does today. The manager, his family and servants, lived over the bank, which was rebuilt in 1864. Next door to the bank (and occupied by Fields' grocers until relatively recently) was Richard Mosey, a grocer, with one assistant and two apprentices living over the shop. On the southern corner of Old Waste was a draper and silk mercer, and there were two more drapers and a hatter between Old Waste and 'Kemp's Corner'. On that site, demolished in the 1950s for road-widening, John Kemp, bookseller and printer, had his office, where he employed two men and three boys.

On the eastern side of the Market Place most of the shops were considerably smaller. Grouped around the White Swan in the Dings were two gunmakers (one family, Akrill's, still trading on the same site), an eating house, a confectioner's shop, an auctioneer, a flour dealer, and a rope-maker. Between Ladygate and Dyer Lane there were two tallow chandlers, a hairdresser, two boot and shoemakers, a shoe seller, a flour dealer, and a leather currier. Between the King's Head and Toll Gavel there was another large linen draper, John Foster, who had three assistants and three apprentices living on the premises. On one of the most prominent sites in the Market Place, now the Push public house (fig. 9), was the business of James Mould Robinson (see below).

Advertisements show the range of goods and services obtainable in the town in the period. Bakers sold potted meat, pork pies, trifles, and biscuits, as well as bread, flour, and hot rolls every morning. At George Hobson's in the Market Place coffee was roasted on the premises, and many grades of tea could be bought, ranging from four to six shillings per pound according to quality. Yorkshire hams and bacon, butter, cheese, sugar and lard were mentioned in many grocers' advertisements, and at Christmas especially, dried fruits were given particular prominence. Many high-class shops advertised a delivery service to country districts. Household goods were available in abundance: at Clark's ironmongers lamps, grates, gas fittings, baths, garden tools, and paraffin were sold, and a large staff included experienced gas-fitters, bell-hangers, and builders. Samuel Findlater, plumber and glazier, provided facilities for the public to take hot, cold, and shower baths in his shop in Toll Gavel. The advertisements of drapers, milliners, and hatters were often very detailed. Some were aimed at those who wished to be in the forefront of fashion: Donkin's in the Market Place offered 'leading novelties in felt hats of every description', whilst S. Barnett, hatter of Walkergate, sold new hats, and dressed and altered old ones in the 'present fashion'. Several drapers also sold floor coverings, paper hangings, parasols, and umbrellas. The latter were often made or repaired as a side line by hairdressers: all four umbrella-makers listed in the 1867 directory were also hairdressers. Other combinations which may be noted are a draper who was also an insurance agent, a grocer-cum-pawnbroker, and surely the most versatile of all — James Mould Robinson, who was a maltster, sold wines and spirits, brewed beer, both for consumption off and on the premises, dispensed medicines and operated as a surgeon, acted as an insurance agent, and sold corn. In 1851 Robinson lived over the shop, but by 1867 he had moved to a more elevated address in North Bar Without.

Although the Market Place was the centre of retailing activity, shops were spread throughout the town, with most of the other large ones being situated in Toll Gavel and North Bar Within. In 1851 in Toll Gavel there were five butchers, three chemists, two bakers, two grocers, two china shops, two general stores, one wine and spirits shop, one confectioner, one watchmaker, and an ironmonger. In the 19th century the shops' signs could be as attractive as inn signs. Chemists and druggists often advertised themselves with pestles and mortars, but more striking, still *in situ*, and dating from c.1830, is the device of two snakes entwined around the door pillars on no. 44 Toll Gavel, a pharmacist's shop throughout the 19th century. Gardham's grocer's shop, which had been in Toll Gavel since the 1770s, had a golden sugar loaf as its sign, whilst Frederick Bartle's Musical Emporium in North Bar Within had a golden lyre.

Many shops had workshops attached, where goods were made or repaired. In 1865, when a serious fire broke out in Westerby's tallow chandlers in the Market Place, the boiling house, where the fire started, contained vats of fat, 200 dozen candles, and barley and peas. As they do still, many of the shops in the Market Place extended a long way back, giving retailers and traders plenty of room for workshops and storage. Clark's ironmongers carried a large stock of sizeable goods, which it could store easily because its premises stretched back to Lairgate, as does Briggs and Powell's today on the same site.

Some changes in social habits are reflected in the directories. Music-making in the home became more popular in Victorian times, and instruments were more widely available and cheaper. In Beverley in 1851 there was no music shop, but by 1858 Frederick Bartle had opened his Musical Repository in North Bar Within, and by 1867 he had been joined by Joseph Coverdale in Butcher Row. Coverdale advertised violins from 1s 3d, concertinas from 2s 6d, and accordians from 4s. He was able to hire out brass or string bands for balls and parties. Frederick Bartle took music pupils, who often played and performed at concerts in the town.

Another change in retailing was a by-product of the Crimean War, 1854-6, when servicemen were introduced to the smoking of cigarettes by Turkish soldiers. Beverley apparently had no tobacconists in 1851, though tobacco was sold by some grocers, for example James Stephenson of Toll Gavel, whose advertisement stated that he sold 'Leeds tobacco'. The introduction of cigarette smoking may perhaps account for the increase in the number of tobacconists from three in 1858 to seven in 1867, two being in the Market Place. Tobacco pipes were made in Beverley in mid-century: in the 1851 census four pipe-makers are listed. They will all have been making clay pipes, since briars were not introduced until a few years later.

Professional photographers began to appear in Beverley in the 1850s. In 1856 Mrs. Leaf's 'Old Photographic Establishment' was advertised in the *Beverley Guardian*. When she closed her business in 1861 all the portraits were offered at half price, the cheapest and smallest (locket-sized) being six pence. In the same year Winter's Crystal Photographic Studio, Register Square, was advertising full-length portraits for use on visiting cards, and in 1865 Beverlonians could have their portraits taken at Goulding's, Butcher Row, who offered:

> *an entirely new portraiture (invented by ourselves) consisting of three heads on one card, the centre being in fine relief, and when artistically coloured, they are the neatest specimens of Carte de Visite ever introduced to the public.*

To take advantage of the new craze for photographs George Gardham, bookseller, was selling photographic albums in 1866 at prices ranging from sixpence to one guinea.

8 Saturday Market Place, Lithograph by E. H. Buckler, c.1860. (Humberside Arts and Leisure).

9 No. 27 Saturday Market Place (James Mould Robinson's shop in mid-19th century).
(P. A. Crowther).

35

Newsagents and booksellers had become quite numerous by the mid-Victorian period. Beverley's two newspapers, the *Beverley Recorder*, and the *Beverley Guardian*, were established in the mid-1850s, and there may have been more buying and reading of other periodicals as a result of the many educational societies which sprang up in the town in the period. Ward's in Wednesday Market Place sold newspapers, books (including children's picture books), playing cards, birthday and Valentine cards, writing materials, ledgers and account books, and provided a printing service for businesses and personal use. Green's lending library held an up-to-date selection of books. In 1856 he was advertising novels by Dickens, Mrs. Gaskell, and Thackeray within months of their publication.

Retail businesses were many and varied in the mid-Victorian period, but the pace of life was apparently unrushed. A visitor to the town in the early 1860s, Edwin Waugh, walked around the shops early in the working week. He described the grass growing in the Market Place, sparrows feeding on left-overs from market day, and the relaxed attitude of the shopkeepers to customers:

> *Indeed, ... [they] seemed surprised at the sight of a customer, –that is if one happens to succeed, by dint of shouting and kicking the counter, in rousing such a wight from his downy lair, in the rear of the premises. Between breakfast and dinner they seem to have a neighbourly way of sauntering from door to door, bidding one another "good morning", and inquiring about the progress of population in their several households, – that is when the weather is fine; for if it rains, they lean against their doorposts, and talk to one another across the street. And on sunny afternoons they come lounging to their thresholds, now and then, with a slow aldermanic air, like whales rising to blow, and there they bask and yawn, and rub down their well-filled waistcoats, as if they had just awakened from a nap after dinner ... Taken as a whole they have a kind of endowed look; and they seem as if they had all been born with money in the bank, and didn't need to stint the butter on their muffins. ... They are a solid, rotund, respectable, canny, old-fashioned race; broad-fronted and broad-bottomed, and as sleek-skinned as moles; and they open their mild eyes in a quiet way, like well-fed kine chewing their cud ... They hardly seem to know that there is any world outside of their garden-girdled town ...*

Such may have been the shopkeeping class. It seems likely that the manufacturers of Beverley were a little more dynamic. In the mid-Victorian period the town had at least one claim to fame: it was the home of William Crosskill's iron foundry. Other industries also flourished on a modest scale; the town had long been a centre of the tanning industry, and it was also the location for milling, colour, fertiliser and whiting works, and ship-building. Most of those undertakings were located on the eastern side of the town, near Beverley Beck and in the Grovehill area. Beverley Beck, linking the town with the Humber, enabled Beverley to develop a small manufacturing sector. By the beginning of the 19th century the most important exports were leather and malt, whilst coal, building materials, and luxury goods such as wine and spirits, were some of the imports.

The Ordnance Survey map of 1853 shows many industrial buildings in the Beckside area, including warehouses (fig. 10), coal yards, bone yards, two linseed mills, a brick and tile yard, a blue and whiting works, the gas works, a wind-mill and a water-mill, and in Flemingate, two tanneries. The 1851 census records 12 master mariners, 17 watermen and a lock-keeper living in Beckside itself, whilst there were eight persons living on board five vessels moored in the Beck on census night. They included a master mariner with his wife and waterman son. The arrival of the railway in Beverley might have been expected to diminish the importance of the Beck, but the tonnage carried rose rather than fell. Tonnage carried on the Beck was 36,227 in 1858, rising to almost 40,000 in 1868. In 1863, when a new crane was tested in the presence of the mayor and the Beck Committee, it was said that the old cranes, which could only raise five tons, were inadequate 'for the increasing trade'. Income from tolls after 1850 often exceeded £700 per annum. The continuing importance of the Beck was no doubt due to the fact that it was in the charge of the corporation, which recognised its role in the economic life of the town.

The vessels which traded to and from Beverley included Humber keels, which were broad-beamed and square-rigged, some of them actually built in the town. There were in the mid-Victorian period several shipyards building principally river craft. Harrison's and Scarr's were at Beckside, and Haselhurst's at Grovehill. In 1858 the corporation gave permission for a second dry dock to be constructed near the lock on the river for Haselhurst's. The 1851 census shows shipwrights, ships' carpenters, sailmakers and ropemakers working in the town. The launch of a boat, broadside on (as was necessary because of the River Hull's narrowness), was an occasion for a crowd to gather. In March 1860 a carvel-built vessel was launched from Harrison's shipyard, to cheers from the assembled onlookers. The *Beverley Guardian* commented that Beverley was becoming quite an important ship-building port of river craft, 'the three yards in full blast'. In April of the same year Haselhurst's launched a 90-ton clinker-built boat for Dyson, Tindall, and Co. of Hull, and in July Scarr's launched a keel, the fourth vessel to be launched that year.

At Grovehill there were two other large businesses. Pennock Tigar, who began his career as a druggist, had by 1830 established a paint and colour factory on the banks of the river there (fig. 11). In 1851, when Tigar died, the business was sold, and turned over to the manufacture of fertilisers. The other large undertaking was Josiah Crathorne's flour mill, which had an extensive frontage onto the Beverley and Barmston Drain. In May 1858 there was a serious fire at the mill, which at that time consisted of a windmill, to which, reported the *Beverley Guardian*, 'steam is also applicable', together with warehouses to its north and south, an engine house, stables, cart sheds, offices, and Mr. Crathorne's house, an imposing Georgian residence. Despite the efforts of the Beverley fire engine and another from the iron foundry, the sails and fan of the mill collapsed onto the engine room. Apparently that fire was

37

instrumental in the decision to go over fully to steam. In the 1850s corn-milling was an important industry in Beverley, and there were in 1851 and 1858, nine corn millers, including four on Westwood (Table 2). However the 1867 directory records a drop to only four, which may be the effect of the growth of Crathorne's business after the fire. By 1880 only Crathorne's remained.

Owing to the proximity of the chalk Wolds several whiting works operated throughout the period. They were located in Beverley Parks and Beckside. Another extractive industry was brick-making, of which the most important firm was that of Anthony Atkinson, closed in 1865 after 45 years in business. Brewing and malting were also of importance to the town's economy in the mid-Victorian period. There were several large breweries, most notably Johnson's in Ladygate, and the Golden Ball brewery in Toll Gavel. Most breweries malted their own barley, but the Ordnance Survey map of 1853 also shows numerous malt kilns scattered throughout the town.

Tanning and associated leather trades had been practised in Beverley since medieval times. A constant water supply was necessary for the tanning processes, and the town's numerous streams provided it. Tanning could be a smelly business. The first operation in a tannery was to clean the hides, some of which may have come directly from the abattoir. They were next soaked in water to soften the fibres, and then transferred to vats of liquid lime to remove the hair. Steeping time and strength varied according to whether the leather was required for shoe soles (when it needed to be hard) or for harnesses and belts (which required a softer quality). The hides were then stretched over a frame and scraped, after which they were transferred to vats containing progressively stronger solutions of tannin, a product of oak bark. They were suspended from poles so as not to touch one another, and remained in the vats for weeks. Finally the hides were allowed to drip-dry before being passed to the currier, whose job it was to work oil and grease into the leather to make it pliable and increase its strength.

In the middle of the 19th century there were four or five tanneries in Beverley, the largest being that of Richard Hodgson, who employed 70 men at his works in Flemingate. He imported large quantities of foreign hides as well as using local sources: in 1850 his stock in hand included Spanish, German, Dutch, and Irish hides, and in 1852 the weight of leather stored on the premises was stated to be 36,734 pounds, with a further 10,598 pounds on consignment. The 1851 census shows the majority of tannery workers living in the Flemingate area, where there was another tannery, owned by George Catterson, and in Keldgate, where a large tannery, owned by George Cussons, was located. Cussons employed 39 men in 1851. Catterson combined tanning with fellmongering, as did Thomas Waddington of Lairgate whose family went on to establish the leather-working firm of Waddington's of Newland, Hull. The 1851 census lists 284 people working in the leather trade, which included 28 tanners, 69 tanners' labourers, and several fellmongers, skinners, curriers, and saddlers.

The largest employer of labour in the 1850s was the iron foundry of William Crosskill. At the age of 13 in 1814 William Crosskill began his career at a whitesmith apprenticed to his widowed mother at a workshop in Butcher Row.

In 1825 the firm of William Crosskill, whitesmith, brass and iron-founder, was already well-established, and in 1827 it moved to new premises off Mill Lane. In those early years Crosskill manufactured railings, lamp standards, stoves, grates, hothouses and conservatories, but he soon began to move into the design and manufacture of agricultural machinery, for which he was to achieve national recognition. In the late 1830s he produced his celebrated clod-crusher roller, which was awarded prizes and medals by numerous bodies including the Royal Agricultural Society, and received the 'Council Great Medal' at the Great Exhibition in 1851. Crosskill's had made almost 2,500 clod-crushers by the end of 1850. Many more machines, some based on other people's designs, some newly-invented, followed: a portable farm railway for working wet ground, threshing and reaping machines, carts and waggons, even an emigrant's kit, including a plough, harrows, and other tools ready for assembly overseas. The foundry was considerably enlarged, and by 1854 it covered seven acres of land on either side of Mill Lane. Whether by good fortune or design (Crosskill was a councillor) when the railway came to Beverley in 1846 it ran alongside the ironworks, which enabled sidings to be built for the better transportation of the products.

In 1847 over-expansion forced Crosskill to mortgage the business to the East Riding Bank. Nevertheless production continued to expand, and the work-force grew fast, so that by the mid-1850s the firm was employing over 500 men. The Crimean War (1854-6) brought a boom in business, with Crosskill's supplying shells, mortars, and 3,000 carts and waggons, which increased the work-force to 800 at one point. Despite that apparent success, capital was still in short supply, and in 1855 the entire property passed over to the bank as trustee for the creditors, who were owed over £73,000. The firm continued, though William virtually retired from the business leaving the management to his sons, Edmund and Alfred. In 1864 the business was sold, and a new limited company, the Beverley Iron and Waggon Company, was formed. The Crosskill brothers set up a new firm, William Crosskill and Sons, on a site in Eastgate, where they continued in business, mainly concentrating on waggons and carts, until 1904.

The very large scale of the ironworks in the early 1860s is well-described in a contemporary railway guide, with an accompanying engraving (fig. 12):

As we enter the premises the offices are on our left, and on our right is an access to the great show-room for every article made by the firm. Near to this are the large store-rooms. We pass through the grounds to the model-rooms, and turn right to the foundries. Beyond these are yards well stored with pig and scrap iron, etc. Near these is the gas house, where the gas used throughout the works is manufactured by the firm for their own consumption. In the fitting shop will be seen a large collection of valuable machinery, portable engines, etc. The smithy is one of the most complete of its kind, and is furnished with forty-six fires. Near to this the observer will remark with astonishment the immense quantity of bar-iron, coals, etc. The wagon shop is in

10   Brigham's corn warehouse, Beckside. (Stuart Witty).

11   Tigar's colour manufactory, Grovehill. (Stuart Witty).

40

Mill Lane. Here we saw thousands of trenching barrows. Adjacent to this department are the carpenters' shops, filled with circular saws, piling, boring, and drilling machines, all moved by steam power of great force. Passing through a portion of the timber yard, we reach the wheel shops, where may be seen in full activity, boring, turning, facing, and spoke-dressing machines. Near to this is the engine room, containing two enormous engines manufactured by the firm. The sawing department succeeds, with its endless circular and upright saws.

Crosskill's works dominated, but there were other ironworks in Beverley in the 1850s and 1860s, most notably William Sawney's in Trinity Lane. The 1851 census shows a great variety of occupations associated with metal-working, including whitesmiths, founders, moulders, tinners, nail-makers, engineers, mechanics, and millwrights. At that time 250, about seven per cent of the work force of Beverley were thus employed.

Table 2 shows the wide range of other trades and crafts in Beverley in the 1850s and 1860s. Most were of only local importance, catering for the residents of the town and its immediate neighbourhood. One firm which might be singled out for mention is the coach-building business of Puckering and Houlgate, which exhibited, like Crosskill's, at the Great Exhibition of 1851. In that year they were employing four men and eight boys, whilst in 1861, when the firm was called Robert Puckering and Co. 11 men, five apprentices, and one woman were employed. In 1857 they were advertising baby carriages, something of a novelty at that time. They had a rival in 1867, when John Gouldwell opened his Perambulator Manufactory in Old Waste. His basket perambulators sold at prices ranging from 5s 6d, and he also let them out on hire.

Beverley was the centre of an agricultural district, and there were therefore many people working in agriculture-related occupations (Table 3). Many agricultural labourers lived in the town but worked in the surrounding parishes. The extensive commons, where freemen had grazing rights, accounted for the numerous cowkeepers. There were several large nursery gardens, most notably those of Thomas and George Swailes. In 1865 an advertisement announced that the business had been established for over fifty years, and that the nurseries covered over 100 acres, and contained several million forest and fruit trees, a general stock of evergreen and deciduous shrubs, and roses. The 1851 census shows 285 people working in agriculture, and 73 in horticulture; together those two groups accounted for almost ten per cent of the working population.

The town was regarded as a desirable place in which to live, and it therefore attracted a class of resident who could choose their place of abode. The census indicates that in 1851 there were 233 people (five per cent of those with recorded occupations), living on incomes derived from property or investments. The upper and middle classes of Beverley also included professional people — doctors, bankers, lawyers, architects, surveyors, and ministers of church and chapel. For those who could afford their fees Beverley was well-provided with doctors. In 1851 the census recorded five M.D.s and four medical pupils practising in the town. Financial services were provided in 1851 by five banks, increasing to seven by 1867. The Beverley Bank was in North Bar Within, the East Riding Bank was on the corner of Newbegin and Lairgate, the Yorkshire Bank was in the Market Place (now the National Westminster) in a building rebuilt in 1864, the Hull Bank was in Lairgate, and the Savings Bank had been established in 1818 in Hengate, but had moved to its new building in Lairgate (fig. 13) in 1843. It only opened on Saturdays, fair days and during the sittings, and was clearly aimed at the small saver. In the same category were the Post Office Savings Bank, Register Square, and the Penny Savings Bank, Minster Moorgate, which opened on Monday evenings from 6 p.m. to 7 p.m. It was announced in 1865 that £1,257 had been deposited in the Penny Bank since its establishment in 1860. It was 'the poor man's friend' storing 'his small sums, in readiness for rent day'.

A town that was the centre of an agricultural district, and an attractive place of residence, required professional land agents, architects and surveyors, auctioneers and valuers. The number of firms of land agents and surveyors grew from three in 1851 to eight in 1867 (Table 4). The coming of the railway in 1846 seems to have stimulated the building of new houses and terraces: the architect Edward Page, with his son Gregory, was responsible for the layout of Railway Street; William Hawe, who established himself in Beverley in 1842, was responsible for many new buildings, both public and private. Throughout the 1850s and 1860s there were three firms of auctioneers and valuers operating in the town. Legal services were provided by several partnerships of attorneys and solicitors, Lairgate being the favoured street for their offices. In 1851 there were five such firms, rising to eleven in 1867. Insurance agents were numerous in the period: in 1851 there were 17 firms with representatives in the town, rising to 33 in 1867. The agents were usually either shopkeepers or attorneys. There were three or four veterinary surgeons throughout the period, though at that time they will not have possessed recognised qualifications.

No account of the economy of a Victorian town could exclude domestic services. Even modest establishments employed a servant or two. Twenty per cent (788) of the working population in 1851 were domestic servants, and more than half of that number (471), were female general servants, whilst there were 43 cooks, 30 nurses, 46 grooms, and 70 housekeepers, together with governesses, lady's companions, butlers, kitchen maids, footmen, and so on. To those could be added other providers of services, including 60 laundresses, 17 washerwomen, two mangle-keepers, and 24 charwomen listed in the census. More than half the households in Saturday Market Place had at least one living-in servant in 1851. In the late 1850s two servants' register offices were established in Beverley. Many young girls no doubt continued to find places on their own, though higher class, more specialised servants may have made more use of the register offices. A successful professional man, such as Thomas Shepherd, an attorney living in Newbegin, could afford a large staff to cater for the needs of himself and his family: in 1851 a lady's maid, a cook, a housemaid, a nurse, an under-nurse, and a footman lived in his house. Sir William Henry Pennyman, of Lairgate, who was 87 in 1851, lived in lonely style with his niece-in-law, supported by a housekeeper, a cook, a laundrymaid, two housemaids, a kitchenmaid, a butler, and a groom-cum-footman.

TABLE 1   RETAILERS

Type	1851	1858	1867
Bacon factor	1	-	-
Booksellers, printers, stationers	6	5	7
Butchers	20	18	24
Chemists, druggists	7	8	9
China, glass dealers	5	3	2
Clothes dealer	-	-	1
Coal merchants	10	9	11
Confectioners	4	4	5
Corn factors	6	8	7
Fancy repository	-	2	1
Fishmongers, game dealers	2	4	5
Flour dealers	10	12	13
Fruiterers, greengrocers	3	8	7
Furniture broker	-	1	-
Grocers, tea dealers	24	25	17
Ironmongers	5	5	6
Linen, wool drapers	14	13	14
Music sellers	-	1	2
Periodical dealers, newsagents	3	1	5
Picture dealer	-	-	1
Shopkeepers, provision dealers	52	43	69
Silk mercers, haberdashers	7	-	-
Tallow chandlers	3	2	3
Timber merchants	1	2	2
Tobacconists	-	3	7
Toy dealers	2	3	1
Wine and spirit merchants	6	5	6
Wool merchants	2	2	-

TABLE 2   TRADES AND CRAFTS

Type	1851	1858	1867
Agricultural implement and machine-makers	7	6	7
Animal preserver	-	1	-
Axle tree makers	2	1	-
Bakers, flour dealers	9	6	3
Basket makers	5	2	3
Beehive maker	-	-	1
Bird stuffer	-	-	1
Blacksmiths	14	10	5
Boat builders	1	1	2
Book binder	-	1	-
Boot, shoemakers	41	48	39
Braziers, tinners	8	7	8
Brewers, maltsters	10	4	9
Bricklayers, builders	20	13	16
Brickmakers	5	4	3
Brush maker	1	1	1
Cabinet-makers, upholsterers	12	13	11
Carvers, gilders	3	2	1
Coachbuilders	2	3	3
Coopers	4	3	3
Corn millers	9	9	4
Curriers, leather cutters	4	4	4
Dyers	4	2	3
Ginger beer maker	1	-	1
Gunmakers	2	1	2
Hatters, hosiers, glovers	16	12	10
Iron, brass founders, engine, boiler-makers	3	3	2
Joiners, builders	15	11	11
Lime-burner, paint, colour, mustard, cement and whiting manufacturer	4	2	4
Manure manufacturers	-	-	2
Milliners, dressmakers	31	36	35
Mint distiller	1	-	1
Painters	11	11	17
Paper hangers	3	-	-
Patten, clog makers	3	2	1
Pavers	2	1	2
Photographers	-	-	2

12   Crosskill's iron foundry. (G. Measom. **Official illustrated guide to the North-Eastern ... Railway ...,** *1861).*

13   Former Savings Bank, Lairgate. (P. A. Crowther).

TABLE 2   TRADES AND CRAFTS

Type	1851	1858	1867
Plumbers, glaziers	6	6	5
Rope, twine manufacturers	2	3	2
Saddlers	5	6	6
Sawyer	1	1	-
Seedcrushers, bone and rape dust manufacturers	3	3	2
Staymakers	7	4	2
Stone, marble masons	3	5	4
Straw hat makers	6	5	-
Tailors	34	28	26
Tanners	4	3	5
Tobacco-pipe makers	2	1	-
Turners	3	5	3
Umbrella makers	-	2	4
Watch, clock makers, jewellers	7	6	9
Well sinker	1	-	1
Wheelwrights	9	10	3
Whitesmiths, bellhangers	7	6	7
Wire workers	2	-	-

TABLE 3   AGRICULTURE-RELATED OCCUPATIONS

Type	1851	1858	1867
Cattle dealers	3	6	6
Cowkeepers	32	22	30
Farmers	6	7[1]	12
Gardeners and seedsmen	11	13[1]	20
Nurserymen	3	4	3

Notes:

[1] Excluding Beverley Parks.

TABLE 4   SERVICES

Type	1851	1858	1867
Academies	21	21	16
Attorneys	5	7	11
Auctioneers	3	3	3
Bankers	5	5	7
Chimney Sweeps	3	-	2
Eating houses	3	2	3
Fire and life offices	17	13	33
Hairdressers	10	11	11
Inns and taverns	36	42	37
Beerhouses	8	13	25
Land surveyors and agents	4	7	8
Livery stable keepers and Hackney coach proprietors	-	3	5
Lodging houses	1	7	20
Pawnbrokers	2	1	1
Servants' register offices	-	2	3
Surgeons	6	6	10
Veterinary surgeons	4	4	4

Source:

White's directories for 1851, 1858 and 1867

CHAPTER THREE
TRANSPORT AND COMMUNICATIONS

Beverley (fig. 1) was at the centre of a network of roads, most of which were turnpiked from the middle of the 18th century. Turnpiking involved the placing of toll-gates by private trusts near either end of a road, where payments were taken from all those except foot travellers who passed along it. The tolls were used to improve the road surfaces. The system remained in operation until the latter half of the 19th century. Beverley's tollhouses and gates stood on the outskirts of the town: on the White Cross road a little to the west of Hull Bridge, on the York road at Bishop Burton, on the Hessle road just north of Butt Lane, on the Hull road at Woodmansey, and on the Malton and Driffield roads at the junction of Gallows Lane and New Walk (fig. 14). That last tollhouse was described in mid-century as 'small and unsightly', and was probably regarded as unsuitable for an area of such elevated character as New Walk was fast becoming. Partly for that reason, and partly because travellers were avoiding the toll by leaving their vehicles and horses at the Molescroft village inn and walking into Beverley, it was pulled down in 1852 and a new one erected at the junction of the Malton and Driffield roads at Molescroft.

Tolls were always unpopular, but seem to have been accepted as a necessary evil until the 1830s, when an anti-toll association was formed in Hull. In the 1830s and 1840s the rise of the railways began to have an inevitable effect on road traffic. The concern felt by the turnpike trustees at the prospect of competition was shown in October 1844 when a man was stationed by the toll bars on the Hull and Driffield roads to record every vehicle passing through, together with the number of its passengers and the nature of its load. Traffic certainly dropped after 1846, when the railway from Hull to Bridlington was opened, and in 1847 tolls were reduced in response to the competition. Nevertheless the turnpikes survived for another two decades after which responsibility for the roads passed to the parishes.

Perhaps the most interesting vehicles using the roads at the opening of the railway age were the long-distance coaches. It is possible to measure their rise and decline by looking at contemporary directories. In 1840 there were five principal coaching inns in the town — the King's Head and the Green Dragon in Saturday Market Place, and the Beverley Arms, the Tiger and the King's Arms in North Bar Within. The service to Hull (fig. 15) was quite frequent; it was possible to travel there at 8 a.m. by the Highflyer from the King's Head, at 9 a.m. by the Beverlac from the King's Arms, at 10 a.m. by the Mail from the Green Dragon, at 10.15 a.m. by the Mail from the Beverley Arms, at 2 p.m. by the Wellington from the Tiger, at 5 p.m. by the Pilot from the Green Dragon or the Queen Adelaide from the King's Arms, and at 11.30 p.m. by the Old Mail from the Tiger. An omnibus — at that time a word used for any public vehicle for passengers — also ran to Hull every day at 8.30 a.m. A traveller to York could travel by the Trafalgar at 8.30 a.m., or catch the Express, which left Hull at 11 a.m. Both coaches left from the Beverley Arms. The Wellington left the Tiger or the Beverley Arms (they took the business alternately) at 9 a.m. for Scarborough. Those coaches must have provided the inns with a very lucrative business, both in stabling and in entertaining travellers. However in 1847 mail coaches stopped running through Beverley, when the mail began to be carried by train. By 1851, when the Hull-Bridlington railway line had been in operation for five years, there was a considerable diminution of all coaches: the York and Scarborough services were discontinued, and only one coach went to Hull, and that only on a Sunday. Those that remained were very local: one went to Market Weighton daily, one to Hornsea on Mondays and Thursdays and one to Brandesburton on Tuesdays and Saturdays. The stage coaches, with their historic names and liveries, were already things of the past.

Country carriers carried both people and goods, and came in from the country districts each Saturday, which was market day in Beverley. They usually arrived at about 10 a.m. and left at 3 p.m. They too used inns and public houses to drop and pick up passengers. No less than 21 carriers' carts congregated at the Green Dragon in the market place every Saturday in 1851. They came not only from the villages in the immediate vicinity of Beverley but also from as far afield as Wetwang and York. The Globe and the Cross Keys were also very busy on Saturdays: about a dozen carriers used those inns as their headquarters. Other inns used were the Dog and Duck, the Holderness Hotel, the King's Head, the Pack Horse, the Wheat Sheaf, the Lion and Lamb, the Valiant Soldier, and the White Horse. The carriers stabled their horses at the backs of the inns, leaving their carts in the Market Place to use as makeshift stalls (fig. 5).

The streets must have been rather congested on Saturdays and the letter printed in the *Beverley Guardian* in October 1856 suggests that not every one observed the 19th century equivalent of the highway code. The writer, who signed himself 'A Barrister', criticised the negligence and inattention displayed by those in charge of heavy waggons and covered vans, which occupied the centre of the road, and made so much noise that the drivers did not hear any call from behind to move over. For the benefit of such road hogs the writer itemised the rules of correct behaviour on the road, which demanded that the driver was never so far way from his carriage that he could not have 'the direction or government of his horses', that he should never leave the vehicle on the highway so as to obstruct the passage of others, should always keep to the left when meeting other waggons, and should not drive two carts at once. Road accidents were commonplace: the newspapers are full of stories of runaway horses, upset carts and carriages, and colliding vehicles. Horses were easily startled and could cause serious accidents. In 1858 at the Molescroft toll bar, a horse was startled by a 'whirlygig' which had been placed on a chimney pot to improve the draught. In 1869 a groom at the King's Arms was killed by the kick of a horse and a butcher's daughter was killed in the same year by a coach overturning. Relatively minor accidents could have quite serious consequences at a time when medical science was somewhat primitive and broken limbs could result in permanent disability.

The vehicles to be seen on the streets were quite varied. The tolls taken on turnpike roads depended on the type of vehicle, and by the mid-19th century a typical list of passenger-carrying vehicles listed in tables of tolls could include coach, chariot, post chaise, landau, berlin, phaeton, sociable, vis-à-vis, curricle, and diligence. Most of those would have been owned by the upper classes. However, in Beverley, a market town and the centre of an agricultural district, the more plebeian vehicles, such as omnibuses, carriers' carts, waggons, waggonettes, gigs, pony carts, and drays, were probably more commonly seen on the streets. Those vehicles, and the horses which provided the motive power, kept an army of people busy in the town. The larger houses, the inns, and the commercial premises, had stables attached to them. Grooms, stable lads, coachmen, draymen, cab proprietors, cart men, horsebreakers, farriers, and other staff, were employed in large numbers. Many people were employed in the making and mending of vehicles.

The railway age began for Beverley in 1846 when the line from Hull to Bridlington opened, but a link between Hull and the town had been contemplated earlier. Anthony Atkinson, the mayor of Beverley, was invited to the opening of the Hull-Selby line in 1840. Responding to a toast he mentioned that a line from Hull to Beverley was under discussion, and he suggested, perhaps rather tactlessly, that such a line might induce many Hull gentlemen to move to Beverley for the sake of their health. Apparently that projected line was to terminate at Beverley, either in St. John's Street near the Minster, or in Well Lane. In the event, and more logically, the line that was built ran to Bridlington, linking with another from that town to Scarborough, constructed in the same period.

The prospect of a railway line between Beverley and Hull was not greeted with enthusiasm by all. There were several groups of people whose livelihoods were threatened by the railways. The turnpike trustees naturally viewed the prospect of rivals with dismay. Coach operators' business might be expected to decline dramatically after the railway line was built. Innkeepers were also concerned that their businesses would suffer. Opposition to railways also came from landowners, farmers and country gentlemen for a variety of reasons: their farms might be divided; natural drainage channels could be interrupted; secluded estates could lose their privacy; hunting might be affected; land values decreased; livestock disturbed by the black smoking monsters racing through fields; sparks from the engines might start fires. It was natural for people to view the innovation with considerable misgivings. The general public expressed anxiety at the prospect of having to cross railway lines. In a Leeds newspaper in 1825 it was suggested in all seriousness that it might be desirable to build hospitals every five miles or so along lines to care for the victims of accidents!

Some of those anxieties were expressed in 1845 in Beverley. In January of that year the projected railway was discussed at a meeting of the town council. The principal worry at that meeting was the necessity of the line crossing Flemingate on the level. It was stated that never before had Parliament sanctioned a line passing over a street in the centre of a town. The opposition was led by Councillor James Mould Robinson, who said that a bridge must be provided. He said that it was the duty of the corporation to protect the lives and property of the inhabitants of Beverley 'and to resist an innovation and a

14   Toll bar at New Walk. Luke Clennell, c.1835. (East Yorkshire Borough of Beverley Borough Council).

15   Coaches in Eastgate. Luke Clennell, c.1835. (East Yorkshire Borough of Beverley Borough Council).

nuisance which will continue as long as the town exists'. Daniel Boyes, who regarded himself as in favour of progress, could see no more danger in such a crossing than there was in a coach crossing, and suggested that in less than three months after the line had been opened 'all would go on as regular as before'. The location of the railway station was also discussed. There had been no definite decision, but the fields to the east of the town known as the Trinities were being suggested as a site. That area belonged to the council, and had been let to Tindalls', the market gardeners, on a 21-year lease since 1824. There was a vote on the railway after the debate at the council meeting, and only two councillors voted against the construction of a line.

The following week a public meeting was held in the Guildhall, which was crowded for the occasion. William Brigham, a seed and corn dealer, moved that the proposed railway would injure Beverley's trade, and might cause taxes to be raised. Councillor Robinson went further, and suggested that the retail trade of the town would be destroyed, taxes would rise and property would depreciate. Councillor Robinson had good reason to be worried about the retail trade since he traded as a brewer and maltster, a chemist and druggist, a surgeon, a corn factor, and a wine and spirit merchant. Many were concerned also about the effect that the railway would have upon the trade carried by water via the Beck.

A director of the Hull and Selby Railway Line, J. R. Pease, put the case for the railway and was supported by Pennock Tigar, the owner of the colour manufactory at Grovehill, who argued that the railway would create a demand for more labour, and for more houses, would increase investment in the town, and would lower the poor rates. William Crosskill, the ironfounder, not surprisingly agreed with Tigar and Pease. He was to find his works in Mill Lane very conveniently situated when the station was subsequently built on the Trinities. He may indeed have had some influence in its siting there, being a councillor at the time. Tigar's amendment to Brigham's motion, that the railway would benefit the town and that the line should pass over Flemingate on the level, was passed with only ten people dissenting.

In February 1846 the Trinities site was valued, and in April the council agreed to sell it to the railway company for £400 an acre. According to the *Hull Advertiser* Beverlonians were getting excited by the prospect of the new line. It suggested that Beverley would be transformed by the erection of manufactories on the eastern side whilst fashionable villas would appear on the west. In May the work on the line had begun, but there were apparently difficulties over land purchase. It was stated in the newspaper that 'so tardy are some of the landowners in giving up possession that the workmen have taken it by force and retaken it several times'. The site of the station was already staked out. The building was expected to be 'an elegant affair ... replete with every convenience'. In June it was announced that the railway line would open in August. An engine was already passing up and down the line between Hull and Beverley 'and the quiet folks of Beverley are almost frightened out of their propriety by the shrill whistles and rumbling of truck wagons' The architect of Beverley's railway station, as of many on the Hull-Bridlington line, was G. T. Andrews. He designed a station with an imposing frontage (fig. 16). The approach was to be from Wednesday Market Place by means of a handsome new street lined with large terraced houses. Two houses would need to be removed to create the entrance from Wednesday Market, which 'spacious area', said the *Hull Advertiser*, 'will certainly form a most eligible and commanding entrance'.

By July the ironwork for the station had arrived and was being erected. In August work was a little behind schedule, but the line was in place and a train with engineers and contractors made an experimental journey from Hull to Bridlington. At Beverley the train stopped and the workmen on the line and at the station were 'regaled with an abundance of cheese, bread and ale' and entertained by the Beverley Ironworks brass band. All was not celebration however, and even before the official opening of the line Councillor Robinson must have felt that his prophecies were being fulfilled, for there were two accidents in late September: a railway worker had his head crushed between buffers; and a when a cow strayed on the line near Cottingham a man who tried to drive it off fell across the line himself and had his leg crushed by a passing engine.

The official opening took place on October 2nd. Over one thousand people were invited to the celebrations, which took place in Hull, in Bridlington, and en route between the two termini. The members of Beverley Town Council were invited to attend. Representatives of the corporations of Hull, Beverley, and York, were joined by representatives of Trinity House, the Dock Company, the Commercial Chamber, and others. The official train was supposed to leave Hull at 10.30 a.m. but there was a delay of three quarters of an hour because the train from York bearing the York directors, and most notably the 'Railway King', George Hudson, was late. Finally at ten to eleven the train, comprising three engines (named Ariel, Antelope, and Hudson), pulling 66 carriages left Hull station. According to the *Advertiser* the rain fell in torrents, but many people were undeterred and crowds were waiting at every station to see the train. At Beverley, Driffield, and Bridlington bands entertained the crowds. The reaction of country people to the train may be exemplified by a Nafferton couple, Reuben and Sarah Stabler, who went to see the first train through their village: 'We went doon ti see train, an' there was sikan a lot of us; an' when it comed we all lifted up wer airms an' scream'd. Why! t'world's to'nd upshad doon sen then'.

The journey from Hull to Bridlington was performed in two hours, with stops at Cottingham, Beverley, and Driffield to pick up favoured passengers. A lunch for 900 people, described as 'sumptuous' by the *Advertiser*, was provided in the goods station at Bridlington. There were numerous toasts and speeches. The chairman of the company, George Hudson, hoped that the line would bring prosperity to Bridlington and be the means of conveying thousands 'to a place where invigorating breezes would bestow health and long life'. The response on behalf of the inhabitants anticipated (in vain) a time when the town would become an important port for the produce of the Baltic, Holland, and other places. After walking about the town for an hour or two the travellers returned to Hull, and proceeded to a dinner at the Public Rooms in Jarratt Street. The opening of the line was the occasion for a general holiday in

Beverley. Shops closed, bands played throughout the day and there was a public dinner in the afternoon, followed by an evening ball.

The new line seems to have been well-used by Beverlonians from the start. Perhaps the first occasion when it was really appreciated was Hull Fair week. The *Hull Advertiser* recorded on October 16, 1846 that the railway company had advertised that people going to Hull for the fair could travel there and back for one fare. Over one thousand people from all the stations on the line took up that offer and some of the trains were seriously overloaded. At Driffield over 200 people were waiting for the train on Monday morning, and finding it already full a number of people scrambled up on to the tops of the carriages, and the train was delayed until they came down. The *Hull Advertiser* recorded that to cope with the demand:

> *train after train was despatched from Hull to Beverley, and filled as quickly as they arrived. Numbers remained on the platform from the departure of one train to another, but ... the boldest and most determined found room in the carriages while the weak and delicate, even after the departure of the third train, remained unaccommodated. Some set off on foot, and had there been coaches or buses many would have availed themselves of any mode of conveyance. At Hull, the departure of trains with so many persons unaccustomed to a railway station, was a matter of difficulty for station officials, the chief puzzle being the provision of carriages, engines, engineers, and guards, who were made to do double duty.*

Fortunately no-one was hurt in the chaos, despite what the *Hull Advertiser* referred to, rather alarmingly, as the *inexperience* of the officials. The company also offered to new passengers a cheap trip to Bridlington in mid-October: the train left Hull at 7 a.m., and Bridlington at 5 p.m. The return fare was four shillings first class, three shillings second, and two shillings third. The tickets were sold in advance but unfortunately, owing to the inclement weather the excursion was not very well-subscribed. However there were to be many more successful ones in later years.

The construction of the railway changed the face of Beverley in the vicinity of the station and line. The station still exists relatively unchanged externally, except for the remodelling of the front entrance. The facilities included a large booking office, a refreshment room for the first and second class passengers, and separate waiting rooms for first and second class passengers and for ladies, with various offices, storage rooms and coal sheds.

The new street leading from Wednesday Market Place, first known as Railroad Street, by 1861 was called Albert Street (perhaps to raise its tone), finally becoming Railway Street (perhaps because people persisted in calling it so). The Beverley architects Edward and Gregory Page designed the houses, and Gregory lived in the largest, no. 13 (fig. 17). He appears to have been one of the earliest residents in the new street since he is listed as living there in the census of 1851, but next to him are 'four houses building'. The street does not seem to have been such an ornament to Beverley as was hoped. The surface

16   Railway station. (P. A. Crowther).

17   Railway Street. (P. A. Crowther).

left much to be desired, because the council disputed with the railway company whose responsibility it was to make up the pavement. The dispute lasted several years, and there were many complaints in the newspapers about the approach to the station. A letter to the editor of the *Hull Advertiser* in 1851 described the writer's arrival at Beverley where he noticed several 'well-dressed ladies' leave the station and endeavour to walk down the 'abominably dirty footpath ... the entire length of which was dotted with pools of mud'.

The houses in Railway Street were not the only ones to be constructed in connection with the railway: in Trinity Lane, Railway Terrace was built (and still remains). In 1861 ten families were living there, though only William Hitching, a railway ticket collector, was an employee of the railway company. A public house with the name of the Railway soon appeared in Highgate, but under that name it seems to have been rather short-lived.

When the Hull-Bridlington line first opened there were four trains per day each way. In addition to those trains there was an extra train on Tuesdays and Saturdays, which were market days in Hull. Market trains ran from Beverley at 8 a.m. and returned from Hull at 4 p.m. On Sundays a train ran from Hull to Bridlington at 7.30 a.m. and one ran back from the resort to Hull at 4 p.m. Clearly no-one was expected to travel to Hull from Bridlington for a Sunday outing. As time went by trains became more frequent, and a timetable of 1858 (fig. 18) demonstrates how long it took to travel from one station to another, and how many more stations there were on the line than at the present day. The journey from Hull to Cottingham took 10 minutes compared with about 7 minutes today, and that to Beverley took 24 minutes, compared with about 14 minutes today. From Hull to Scarborough took almost three hours, for what is now a journey of one and a half hours.

In 1865, two decades after it was first projected, a branch line from Beverley to Market Weighton was opened, thus allowing Beverlonians to travel direct to York without going into Hull and out again. The delay in building the line had been caused by difficulties with land purchase and problems with the terrain. In September 1863 the first sod was turned, in a field near Cherry Burton, by the local lord of the manor. The ceremony was reported in the *Beverley Guardian*, but seems to have been very low key, being watched by only 'about a dozen stalwart navvies, anxious to begin work, and three or four tradesmen from Beverley'. When the line opened in 1865, Beverlonians soon began to take advantage of it for trips to York, among them being Beverley Oddfellows, who had an outing to the city shortly after it was opened.

The rolling stock used in the mid-19th century presented a colourful sight. The engines and carriages were brightly painted, and the combination of their colourful livery and the noise, steam, and smoke must have made a great impact on country people round about. There was considerable difference in the standards of accommodation in the classes (see drawing of train at top of fig. 18), and a contemporary account of the early days of railways on the Hull to Bridlington line in a book by the Reverend M. C. F. Morris of Nunburnholme is worth quoting:

... the firsts, ... were pretty much the same as now [early 20th

century] save for the lighting, heating, and height. The second classes were closed up to the top, but there were no cushions whatever, either on the seats or backs. The thirds were not much inferior to the seconds, only that the divisions of the compartments did not extend much higher than the shoulders of the passengers when seated; so that you could see the heads of the travellers through the entire length of the carriage. Then there were carriages which were more like cattle trucks than anything else. These had no tops, and no divisions, but only a few seats or benches to sit upon. These we used to call 'fourths', though I do not think they were designated so by the companies. They were only endurable in summer weather. If it rained you got drenched ... if it blew, as it invariably did, owing to the pace of the train, your hat had to be securely fastened, else you would probably lose it.

(M. C. F. Morris, *Yorkshire reminiscences* (1922))

On the subject of hats there is a reference in an account of the early days of the Hull railways by Macturk to the travellers' habit of putting their heads outside the train to look forward or back along the line, only to lose their hats in the draught. As a result, hundreds of hats were picked up along the line. The third class passengers, being open to the elements anyway, were advised in Fowler's *Railway travellers' guide*, published in Leeds in 1838, to fasten their hats by a ribbon to prevent them being blown off. The same guide included the advice 'to prevent accidents, passengers are warned to keep their seats when the trains are starting, going, or stopping, and invariably to get in and out of the left side of the carriages lest they be knocked down by a passing train'.

The lighting in carriages was 'of the most meagre character, one dingy colza [rape seed] oil lamp fixed between two compartments' whilst the heating was either non-existent or negligible. Luggage was stowed on the tops of those carriages which were enclosed. Apparently porters had to be watched carefully or they would throw the luggage right over the top of the carriage to fall on the line on the other side.

None of the early carriages had corridors and not all of them were lit at night, which made women travelling alone somewhat vulnerable. That is illustrated by a case reported in the *Hull Advertiser* in January 1853 when a Mrs. Duffill, the wife of a Beverley innkeeper, was found lying on the line in 'an insensible state' near Cottingham station. She had been travelling back from Hull at night, apparently in an unlit carriage, with a man from Beverley who was said to have assaulted her and either pushed her on to the line or forced her to jump out of the carriage to escape his attentions. She died a week later. Another aspect of the lack of facilities on early trains on the Hull to Beverley line is illustrated by a charge of indecent conduct brought in 1867 against William Kime, a middle-aged man from Lincolnshire. The Beverley station master and the porter, told the magistrates how when the 1.45 p.m. train from Bridlington arrived the defendant opened the door of a third class compartment and 'made indecent exposure and committed a nuisance on the platform'. Kime's defence was that he had been drinking and was 'desperate'. He was told that he should have left the train at Arram, presumably to relieve himself, and then quickly get back on. He was fined ten shillings including costs.

The impact of railways on the area was considerable, and not always beneficial. Unfortunately those who had feared that the railway would be the cause of injuries and even deaths were soon justified in their fears. There were several fatalities on the line shortly after it opened, usually caused by carelessness on the part of people who were unused to the new form of transport. Railway workers were the most frequent victims of accidents, especially in the early months of operation. Animals seem to have been able to stray upon the line relatively easily, and there are several reports of accidents to livestock. Where the railway lines passed over streets, accidents were particularly common. In 1852 several people waiting at the Grovehill crossing were knocked down by a train which had been left in the charge of the stoker. Somehow it 'dashed off the end of the side line', knocking part of a wall and two gate posts down, and ploughing into the crowd. In 1861 the gatekeeper at Flemingate was killed as a result of a collision with a train and in 1868 one of the crossing gates was torn off its hinges by a train. One year later there was another accident on a level crossing when Grace Cunningham Wilson aged 82, described as a pot hawker, was killed by an express train whilst walking over the lines at England Springs crossing. She was lame and deaf as well as old and apparently failed to hear the approaching train. In 1870 an excursion train from Hull to Whitby ran into the Flemingate gates, seriously injuring the gatekeeper.

The dangerous nature of railways was recognised in an advert placed regularly in the *Beverley Guardian* in the 1860s. It said that six pounds per week could be secured whilst a person was laid up as a result of injury in an accident of any kind, and £1,000 for death, by an annual payment of from £3 to £6 5s to the Railway Passengers' Assurance Company. Passengers could also insure themselves against railway accidents for individual single or return journeys.

The impact that the railways made upon other forms of transport was variable. Certainly the coaches were badly affected, but the railway probably helped the carriers' businesses to some extent, since people in most of the outlying villages had to get to Beverley before they could catch a train, and many would have used the carriers' carts for that purpose. Moreover the railways were not without their critics: in 1850 an item in the *Hull Advertiser* said that light horse vans were about to start up in the Beverley area owing to the high rail prices, whilst in March 1856 a leader in the *Beverley Guardian* discussed the complaints that had been made about the poor train service, and went on, 'We are not so attached to the North Eastern as to abstain from the use of horse and carriage when they will conveniently convey us to our destination'. In 1858 the Mutual Improvement Society, for its excursion, chose:

> the coach-and-four system [in preference] to a railway trip, with uncomfortable hard-seated carriages, shrill whistle, and noxious smoke, and nasty quick jolting motion, leaving the traveller no time to enjoy the pleasant scenery ... while there is something

Railway Time Tables.

FROM SCARBRO' TO HULL.

Stations. LEAVE.	1 (a.m.)	2 (a.m.)	3 (a.m.)	4 (a.m.)	5 (p.m.)	6 (p.m.)	7 (p.m.)	8 (p.m.)	Sun (p.m.)
Scarbro'	6 25	8 0		11 25			4 30	6 0	3 15
Seamer	6 32	8 10		11 32			4 37	6 7	3 22
Cayton	6 38	..		11 37			..	6 13	3 28
Gristhorpe	6 42	..		11 42			..	6 17	3 32
Filey	6 50	8 25		11 48			4 50	6 25	3 40
Hunmanby	6 58	..		11 56			..	6 33	3 48
Speeton	7 8	..		..			..	6 43	3 58
Bempton	7 18	..		12 14			..	6 53	4 8
Martn-Flambro'	7 23	8 45		12 18			5 12	6 58	4 13
Bridlington Arr.	7 31	8 55		12 25			5 20	7 6	4 21
Do. ..Dep.	7 37	9 0		12 34			5 25	7 12	4 27
Carnaby	7 42	..		..			..	7 17	4 32
Burton Agnes	7 49	..		12 43			..	7 24	4 39
Lowthorpe	7 55	..		12 51			5 40	7 30	4 45
Nafferton	8 0	..		12 57			..	7 35	4 50
Driffield	8 13	9 20		1 2			5 51	7 43	4 58
Huttn Cranswk	8 23			1 10			..	7 53	5 8
Lockington	8 31	..		1 18			..	8 1	5 16
Arram	8 37	..		..			..	8 6	5 21
Beverley	8 53	9 40	11 30	1 35	2 30	5 0	6 16	8 20	5 35
Cottingham	9 3	..	11 40	1 48	2 40	5 10	6 26	8 30	5 45
Hull ......Arr.	9 20	10 0	11 55	2 0	2 55	5 25	6 40	8 45	6 0

*** On Tuesdays a Train will leave Beverley for Hull at 8-45 a.m., and in the Afternoon of the same day a Train will leave Hull at 4-20 p.m., for Bridlington and intermediate Stations.

FROM HULL TO SCARBRO'.

Stations. LEAVE.	1 (a.m.)	2 (a.m.)	3 (a.m.)	4 (p.m.)	5 (p.m.)	6 (p.m.)	7 (p.m.)	8 (p.m.)	Sun (a.m.)
Hull	6 20	10 30	11 0	12 30	2 0	4 15	4 30	7 10	7 0
Cottingham	6 30	10 39	11 10	12 39	2 10	..	4 40	7 20	7 10
Beverley	6 44	10 54	11 20	12 54	2 20	4 31	4 50	7 34	7 24
Arram	6 50	10 59		12 59				7 40	7 30
Lockington	6 57	11 5		1 5				7 50	7 40
Huttn Cranswk	7 5	11 18		1 13				8 0	7 46
Driffield	7 16	11 25		1 25		4 56		8 10	8 0
Nafferton	7 22	11 30		1 30		..		8 15	8 5
Lowthorpe	7 27	11 35		1 35		..		8 20	8 10
Burton Agnes	7 33	11 40		1 40		..		8 25	8 15
Carnaby	7 40	11 48		1 48		..		8 31	8 21
Bridlington Arr.	7 50	12 0		1 55		5 19		8 40	8 30
Do. ..Dep	8 0	1 0		2 5		5 24		8 45	8 35
Martn- Flambro	8 7	1 7		2 12		5 29		8 53	8 42
Bempton	8 12			2 18		5 35		8 57	8 46
Speeton	8 19	..		2 25		5 42		9 6	8 55
Hunmanby	8 29			2 35		5 52		9 16	9 5
Filey	8 36	1 30		2 43		6 0		9 24	9 13
Gristhorpe	8 43	..		2 50		6 7		9 30	9 20
Cayton	8 50			2 56		6 13		9 36	9 26
Seamer	8 59	1 43		3 3		6 20		9 43	9 33
Scarbro' ..Arr.	9 10	1 55		3 15		6 32		9 55	9 45

18   Railway timetable. **Beverley Guardian**, 1863. (Humberside Arts and Leisure).

*indescribably jolly in the very idea of being on top of a coach ...
with ever and anon the cheerful note of the post horn saluting
one's ear, causing the healthy and happy rustic to rest on his hay
fork while the cavalcade passes, thinking with regret on the good
old times.*

Road and rail could co-operate very profitably, and the railways must have
had the effect of stimulating more travel, to the eventual benefit of the road
interest. Certainly the two largest inns, the Beverley Arms and the King's Head,
soon began an omnibus service to meet travellers off all trains.

The railway companies seem to have been quite responsive to demand. In
1857 the *Beverley Guardian* carried an editorial calling for more trains in the
summer months, and also requesting the directors to put on a later train from
Hull to Beverley than the 7.30 p.m., which at that time was the last train of the
evening. Apparently that was soon done and on the occasion of performances
at the Theatre Royal, and in the pantomime season, extra late evening trains
were provided. Sunday Schools began to take advantage of the trains to reach
the seaside: the processions of waggons and carriages were replaced by rail
excursions, no doubt to the children's satisfaction. In 1851 people from all over
England went by train to the Great Exhibition, and Beverlonians were no
exception. A public meeting was held on January 1st 1851 to organise cheap
travel to the Exhibition. Clubs to save up the fare were established in the town.

In Kemp's *Beverley guide ...* (1847) the author expressed the opinion that the
new railway line will afford 'facilities for communication and transport not
before enjoyed, which will, no doubt, tend to increase the business of the fairs
and markets, if it do not improve the general trade of the place in other
respects'. He also expressed the hope that it would be the means of more people
coming to see the Minster 'which, were there nothing else in the town worthy of
notice, would amply repay them for their cost and trouble'. Those hopes were
probably fulfilled. The town's trade and industry came to depend upon its
railway lines, while Beverley, being widely recognised as an attractive place to
live, began to develop a role as a 'dormitory town' as a result of its improved
links with Hull. For a century the town was to find its railway line essential for
the transport of goods and passengers.

In the early 1850s Beverley's post office was at first in Toll Gavel,
subsequently moving into premises in Cross Street (until recently Pottage's).
That building was small and dissatisfaction was expressed with the doorway,
which was 'so low that a tall person, if he did not stoop, ran the risk of breaking
his hat'. The building was described as 'no better than a hovel, hardly fit for a
cow house'. The Post Office refused to buy property, but agreed to rent if
suitable premises could be found. In June 1866 a building across the road on
the site of the present County Hall was taken. It was described as
'commodious', and had separate windows for the sale of stamps, money
orders, Savings Bank and insurance, allowing private business to be conducted
'with some degree of security and convenience'.

The postmaster from 1846 until 1858 was Michael Ellis, a printer,
bookbinder and newsagent, who had succeeded his father in the position. At

that time the staff consisted of the postmaster, the clerk, two letter carriers and two rural messengers. Working with quite large sums of money was clearly a temptation, for Ellis was removed from office for being in default for £97, and the next postmaster, William Tilson, was charged with unlawfully opening letters and embezzlement in 1864. He pleaded guilty, and revealed that he had been in financial difficulties and had taken money to try to increase it by betting. At his trial several prominent citizens spoke up for him, but he was sent to prison for six years. The next postmaster, Luke Hind, was found to be in debt, and was removed from office as unsuitable, to be replaced by George Whiting, who remained in office for 15 years.

From 1847, shortly after the railway came to the town, mail, went by rail from Beverley in all directions. In 1856 it arrived from London and from Hull at 8 a.m. and the carriers went out immediately, unless it was to be collected at the post office window. There was another delivery at 5.15, and the carriers went out again. The country carriers went out every morning to deliver mail to the villages round about and returned with their mail every evening about 5 p.m. On Sundays there was only one delivery by letter carriers commencing at 8 a.m.

In 1857 there were two letter carriers, one 'footpost', and four country messengers. On 30th June 1857 the *Beverley Guardian* carried an item:

> *Great discontent prevails amongst the tradesmen of Beverley regarding the recent alterations in the delivery of letters. By the present arrangements all the rural district letters for the town, in addition to those from Bridlington, Driffield, Lowthorpe, are kept at the Post Office until the following day, thus causing a delay of 36 hours in answering correspondence.*

That may have been rectified at the time, but in 1867 there were more complaints because a change in the afternoon delivery had meant that tradesmen were not receiving orders from the country on the day that they were sent. They could not therefore dispatch orders immediately as had been their practice. An indication that postal deliveries were somewhat more frequent than at the present day comes from a newspaper report of December 26 1857:

> *Whilst many a family is enjoying comfortably at home the blaze of the Yule log and Christmas cheer, the postman will be trudging on his way, mayhap in wind and rain, or snow, the bearer of congratulations from their friends.*

Valentine cards too were being sent to loved ones in the mid-Victorian period. In 1865 the *Beverley Guardian* reported that on 14th February 'those connected with the Post Office ... were extremely active ... as nearly 3,000 letters passed through the establishment that day, a number far exceeding previous occasions'.

From 1864 Beverley had its own telegraph office, which was opened first in the architect, William Hawe's office in Register Square. In 1870 it was taken over by the Post Office.

CHAPTER FOUR
LAW AND ORDER

Beverley seems to have been a fairly law-abiding place in the mid-Victorian period, although its markets, fairs, and other festivities attracted undesirable characters at certain times of the year. The borough police force came under government scrutiny in the 1850s, and was found wanting. It was expanded in the early 1860s, and the town succeeded in obtaining a government grant, despite the reluctance of some Beverlonians to accept government involvement. Beverley had its own borough court, which dealt with petty crimes. It was also the centre of justice for the Riding, the East Riding Sessions House being situated in the town (fig. 19). Crimes committed in Beverley ran the gamut from murder and riot to the more common misdemeanours such as drunkenness and petty theft. Punishments ranged from fines to imprisonment with hard labour on the tread-mill in the House of Correction. Crimes carrying the death penalty were tried in York.

The borough police force in the early 1850s consisted of a superintendent, who was also the inspector of nuisances and common lodging houses and collector of the watch rate, eight constables-cum-night watchmen, and three serjeants at mace, who policed the town in the day time. The force had been set up under the Municipal Corporations Act of 1835, and was overseen by the Watch Committee. In 1856 Parliament passed the County and Borough Police Act, which required boroughs to submit their police forces to government inspection, whilst providing them with one quarter of the cost of pay and clothing if they were deemed to be efficient in regard to numbers and discipline. Chief constables were required to report annually to the Home Secretary on the state of crime in the area.

Such interference by central government was not popular. At a meeting held in the Guildhall to consider the Police Bill the mayor said that it was an attempt to vest the whole control of the police in the hands of the state. It was agreed that Beverley was quite competent to manage its own affairs — 'What could the gentlemen in Whitehall know about Beverley?'. At present the only day-time policeman 'could hardly find anything to do'. Particular exception was taken to the idea of the Home Secretary concerning himself with Beverley policemen's uniform — 'Did he suppose we have no tailors in Beverley?'. A resolution that the bill would interfere with the liberties of the subject was carried unanimously, but the Act was passed all the same. The borough's complacency was not shared by the government: an inspector visited Beverley in 1857 and reported that the police force was not up to standard and the town would therefore get no grant. The Watch Committee decided to give Inspector Holden, the Superintendent of the Police, three months' notice, despite many protests from his friends on the council. The *Beverley Guardian* carried an editorial complaining of the unfair treatment of Holden, and when he left he was entertained in the Assembly Rooms and presented with a glowing testimonial from his supporters.

In 1860 the duties of the police and the constitution of the force were described by Superintendent Dove, who had succeeded Inspector Holden. Dove was in overall charge, and during his tour of duty visited each part of the town daily and each nightwatchman twice a week. Saturday was his busiest night when he rarely went off duty before 2 a.m. He was paid £80 per annum. The sergeant, Richard Dunn, was in charge at night, starting at 11 p.m. and going off duty at 6 a.m. He visited each beat twice nightly and was paid 19 shillings per week in winter, and 17 shillings in summer. There were six nightwatchmen, and one supernumerary to fill in if anyone fell ill. Their duties included lighting and extinguishing the public lamps, and cleaning them once a week. They began their lamp-lighting duties at dusk and then went off duty until 11 p.m. when their first duty was to extinguish the lamps. They were then expected to walk their beats from that time until dawn. They also paraded in New Walk from 6.30 to 9.00 every Sunday evening. They were paid 16 shillings per week in winter, and 14 shillings in summer. There were two day policemen who went on duty when the nightwatchmen came off. They were paid £1 per week. There was a goaler, who was also a police officer. His duties included attending the mayor and officiating at corporation meetings. The force was augmented by four unpaid constables.

Apparently that force was still not considered adequate by the government. In January 1861 a report of the Inspector of Police stated that the establishment in Beverley was 'not in accordance with the Act' and moreover was 'totally inefficient'. No attempt had been made to consolidate with the East Riding constabulary (which had been established in 1856 to police the Riding and was organised from the Sessions House). The council disagreed with the report, but in December 1861 Daniel Dove was dismissed and William Pattison appointed. He suggested that the force should be reconstituted, with a sergeant and three constables for day duty, a sergeant and four constables for night duty and one constable to be held in reserve. As a result of those changes Beverley finally got government approval — and the grant — so long as the lamps should cease to be the responsibility of the police. Lamplighting apparently took one and a half hours nightly. The force was divided at that time into first-class constables, experienced men who were paid 19 shillings per week, and second-class constables, who were paid 17 shillings. The sergeants were paid 21 shillings per week. In 1866 increases in pay were made but only by reducing the number of constables to seven, though it was made up to eight again in 1875. A report in 1862 gives the ages of all members of the force. The youngest was 36 and the oldest was 63. Apparently it was not seen as a young man's job.

In the 1820s the watchmen had been supplied by the East Yorkshire Militia with sentry boxes, but by the middle of the century no mention is made of any shelter and the constables were presumably expected to keep on the move. They were supplied with rattles to summon help, and carried lanterns, handcuffs and staves. Little is recorded of their uniform, until in 1856 the inspector asked that the watchmen should be supplied with new capes, and stated that india rubber would be best. In the 1860s tenders were being invited from local shopkeepers for:

> 10 suits of blue uniform clothing, viz.
> 10 great coats
> 10 tunic coats
> 10 pairs of trousers, cloth to be the same as the tunic coats
> 10 silk hats
> 20 pairs of Blucher boots
> 10 pairs of white cotton gloves.

The great coats were described as being 'rug-lined', and they cost £2 3s. Beverley constables apparently wore an identification number, which from 1860 was made of metal.

When the constables arrested someone they took them to the lock-up, which was attached to the Guildhall in Register Square. It had formerly been a borough gaol, but at that period it was used for detaining people on remand and as a place in which drunks could sober up. In the 1860s the Superintendent of Police acted as gaoler and lived in an adjacent house. The gaol contained 14 cells, and three airing yards. Prisoners were placed in separate cells, and provided with a basic diet of eight ounces of bread and a pint of coffee or tea for breakfast and supper, and a pint of gruel and eight ounces of bread for dinner. They were, however, allowed to provide their own food. No tobacco or alcohol was permitted. If charged they had to appear either at the petty sessions or the quarter sessions, according to the nature of their offence.

The petty sessions were held in the Guildhall, sometimes several times a week according to the number of cases. Here were tried the so-called summary offences, which could be tried by two or three magistrates sitting without a jury. In Beverley the mayor was the principal magistrate, and there were six to eight others, chosen from prominent citizens of the town. On the whole summary offences were minor misdemeanours — common assaults, breaches of the peace, drunk and disorderly conduct, vagrancy, poaching and breaches of the licensing laws and local bylaws. After the passage of the Criminal Justice Act of 1855, those accused of petty larceny, that is theft involving goods valued at under five shillings, could be tried at the petty sessions if the accused agreed, whilst thefts of over five shillings could also be heard there if the accused pleaded guilty. More serious offences were indictable, and had to be dealt with either at the quarter sessions before a judge or a bench of magistrates sitting with a jury, or at the assizes before a judge. The quarter sessions tried cases of larceny, house breaking, assault, robbery, or riot. The East Riding Justices of the Peace met at the Sessions House in New Walk for that purpose. The assizes were reserved for those offences for which the death penalty could be imposed (treason and murder), and certain other crimes, including bigamy, bribery, forgery and libel. Other serious indictable offences such as rape, burglary, and robbery with violence were sometimes sent to the assizes, which were held in York.

In a sample six-month period in 1863 the borough magistrates dealt with 105 cases. Almost one quarter (25) were 'drunk and disorderly', 'drunk and vicious', or 'drunk and filthy'. The magistrates fined most of the offenders sums ranging from three shillings to 20 shillings. But two were imprisoned, both of them women. Possibly drunkenness in women was regarded with greater severity by the magistrates. The women received sentences of 14 and 21 days respectively. Two people were discharged on the understanding that they left the town.

There were 16 cases of assault. Several of them were assaults on family members or on neighbours and were mostly dismissed. A fine was the most common punishment, but a 'ticket of leave' convict, who assaulted a man he met in a pub, was sentenced to two months with hard labour, and a man who assaulted a boy shoe-black, who was cleaning his shoes, was sentenced to one month with hard labour. Eight people were accused of theft, of which three were transferred to the quarter sessions, one to Hull, and the remainder were given prison sentences ranging from seven days with a birching for a boy who stole a bale of straw, to 21 days with hard labour for a man who took money from a box placed in the Minster for 'distressed operatives in Lancashire'. Quarrels between neighbours accounted for seven cases. Many of them were dismissed by the Bench. The remaining cases were quite varied. There were two indecent assaults, one involving two boys of ten and eleven who were sent to prison for one month for an indecent assault on a girl of nine. A case in January 1863 concerned four children aged 9, 7, 4 and 3, who were found sitting on a doorstep in Flemingate. Their stepfather had brought them part of the way from Hull, and left them, telling them to go to Beverley workhouse. The magistrates imprisoned the stepfather for one month, regretting that their powers were insufficient to give him more. There were four road traffic offences. Several tramps and vagrants appeared before the court: one was imprisoned for a month with hard labour for breaking 34 panes of glass in the vagrants' ward of the workhouse. An Irish woman with two children was accused of being drunk in the streets. Her submission was that she went to the workhouse but was refused a fire and medical treatment for her sick child. She said that they were more comfortable, and better attended in prison. Three people were accused of offering false coinage. One case concerned cruelty to a cat. Two cases concerned fights between women, described in one case as 'street pests'. There were also four cases of refusal to pay rates of various kinds.

The magistrates remanded those accused of more serious offences to the East Riding quarter sessions, which took place in January, April, July and October. Cases were heard from all over the East Riding, and were divided into cases where the accused had pleaded guilty and those which demanded a trial. At the January sessions in 1863 there were five guilty pleas, whilst six cases came to trial. All concerned either theft or passing false coins. The most severe punishments were imposed upon people with previous convictions: a man who had stolen a bag in Market Weighton was sent for three years penal servitude because he had numerous other convictions, and a woman who had repeated the offence of passing counterfeit coins was sentenced to three months imprisonment, the last 14 days to be spent in solitary confinement. At the April quarter sessions the pattern was the same. By modern standards sentences of ten, six and four years for stealing fowl, all of which sentences were imposed at that court, look very severe indeed. At the July quarter sessions one man was

THE COURT HOUSE, BEVERLEY.

*19   Sessions House, New Walk. (**Beverley guide: being a short account of the principal objects of the town...**, Beverley: John Kemp. 1847).*

*20   Fishwick's Mill. (**Sketches of Beverley and neighbourhood, 1882**).*

sentenced to four years in prison for stealing one shilling and six pence. He had several previous convictions. The chairman of the magistrates expressed satisfaction that 'with one or two exceptions the prisoners were strangers, and did not belong to the Riding'.

A broader view of crime in Beverley throughout the whole period reveals a similar pattern to that shown in the six-month sample period. Drunkenness, and misdemeanours associated with it, seem to have given the Beverley police force much of their employment. The newspapers are full of reports of both men and women disturbing the peace after a convivial night on the town. The *Beverley Guardian* seems to have been particularly assiduous in reporting the misdemeanours of the Irish or the Scots. A report of January 1st 1859 gave a vivid account of one Scotsman's Christmas celebrations:

> *John Smith, a Scotchman and Waterloo veteran, without pension or good conduct medal, was brought up charged with being drunk and disorderly in Lairgate at 1 o'clock on Christmas morning. Smith, it appeared, had been under the command of Sir John Barleycorn, and while in active service became disabled in his limbs, as to require the aid of a brick wall to keep him anything like perpendicular. The strength of his lungs, however, more than made up for the weakness of his limbs, as several persons in the neighbourhood had ample proof in being aroused from their sweet repose. Smith was taken prisoner by Sergeant Dunn, who forthwith conveyed him to the lock-up, where he spent his Christmas. He was fined 5 shillings.*

Drinking places were supposed to shut during the hours of divine services on Sundays, except for *bona fide* travellers. That ruling caused some Beverlonians wanting a drink to travel outside the town. The landlord of the New Inn, Bentley, when charged in June 1856 with keeping his house open during divine service, said that his customers were travellers. One of them, Mr. Martin, a Beverley tailor, stated that he had accompanied a friend who was going to Skidby, and being weary and overtaken by the rain, they went to the inn to ask for shelter and refreshment, which they thought they could legally demand. The Bench decided that persons who resided in Beverley and took a walk of a mile or two for recreation were not *bona fide* travellers. A rather different excuse was given by the landlord of a public house at Walkington. Charged with being open at an improper hour, he said that he went by the clock in the pub, which was 'kept at Walkington time, being about a quarter of an hour before that of Beverley'.

Drunkenness was not the only problem with which the police concerned themselves. Under-age smoking was the occasion of a robbery which took place in 1862. Two boys, aged 13 and 14, were charged with robbing their master, a grocer in Market Place, of tobacco, which they sold to other youngsters, one of whom, Thomas Addy aged 14, when asked if he smoked, replied that he had been a smoker for three or four years. The magistrate sentenced the two boys to 14 days imprisonment, and hoped that the police would watch out for the young smokers 'who were frequently seen in the streets with pipes and cigars in their mouths. Smoking brought on drinking and then gambling and stealing'.

Gambling is mentioned regularly in police reports. In July 1852 the *Hull Advertiser* reported:

> *On Sunday mornings a number of young men and boys make a practice of assembling on Westwood in different groups for the purpose of gambling, by playing cards, dice, brasses, pitch and toss, and other similar games, and also for indulging in the disgraceful and cruel sport of dog-fighting at the same time using the most coarse and foul language.*

In May 1856 some young men were found gambling in St. Mary's churchyard; no doubt many people indulged without being caught.

Dog fights still took place in Beverley in mid-Victorian times, though not with the approval of the magistrates. In 1861 two men set their dogs, a large white mastiff and a small terrier, at each other's throats in Westwood Pits. The mastiff got the terrier by its tongue and would not let go. Its owner lifted it by the tail and swung it round to separate it from the terrier. After that experience the terrier had to be put down. The mayor imposed a fine of £1 with damages of five shillings, remarking that the town was so full of 'fighting, ratting and other dogs as to become a great nuisance, and as probably not one in six of the owners paid the tax on them, dog tax should either be abolished or enforced ...'.

Prize fighting was another sport which was frowned upon, more especially on a Sunday. The *Hull Advertiser* of October 1852 reported a 'disgraceful scene', when two young men met on Westwood 'for the purpose of fighting a pitched battle'. A large crowd assembled to watch. Such fights drew people from a distance: in 1867 a case was brought before the magistrates concerning four men who had organised prize fighting in Beverley Parks, watched by 400 people who had left Hull at 4 a.m. to see the fight. Poaching offences figured in the police reports quite frequently. In February 1867 three Beverley men were caught trespassing in Bentley wood 'in pursuit of game', and also charged with looking for rabbits with two dogs on a farmer's land in Beverley. They were fined ten shillings, plus ten shillings costs.

Today's police force spends a great deal of its time dealing with traffic offences. In the middle of the 19th century such offences were relatively few, but 'furious driving' appears occasionally in court reports. In 1863 a farm servant was charged with driving a waggon and horses so fast along North Bar Street that the pole of his waggon only narrowly missed a dog cart driven in the opposite direction. He was fined £2 plus costs. In 1863 a man appeared before the petty sessions accused of having been drunk in charge of a horse, which he rode in a reckless manner down Toll Gavel, narrowly missing three people. The horse stumbled in Register Square, and the man fell off. He was fined ten shillings. Parking offences also figured in the reports: in 1867 a man was fined one shilling, plus costs of 19s 6d for leaving a horse and cart outside the Prince of Wales beerhouse in Eastgate. His excuse was that he had just come from the gas works and had stopped to wash the gas tar off his hands.

Domestic arguments and family problems brought many people to the attention of the police and the courts. In 1867 a resident of Lurk Lane was brought before the court for beating his wife because his dinner was not ready. It was claimed that he had often beaten her; his excuse was that she neglected the home. He was bound over to keep the peace with a surety of £20. In the same year the landlord of the Anchor Inn, Beckside, came before the court for assaulting his wife by trapping her fingers in a door. He was fined 40 shillings and costs. A case of cruelty to a child caused considerable interest in Beverley in February 1867. The Sessions House was densely crowded for the trial of George and Mary Haldenby of Queensgate. They were accused of starving their son, and flogging him with a leather strap. Neighbours said that he was little more than a skeleton, and that they often fed him themselves. It was claimed that the father beat him almost every night. The charge of starvation was dropped on a surgeon's report that the boy had 'consumption of the bowels', which would account for his emaciation. Mrs. Haldenby was sent to prison for one month with hard labour, but her husband was let off with a fine of 60 shillings.

Quarrels between neighbours often resulted in court attendances. In January 1867 it was stated that Thomas Gamble of Duncan's Yard, Walkergate, had squabbled when drunk, with his neighbour, a Mr. Dixon, and had assaulted him so violently that the case had to be adjourned because Dixon was unable to attend owing to his severe injuries. When the case finally came before the court it was stated that the quarrel began with a fight between the two men's wives using a sweeping brush and a thick stick. The following day the fight flared up again with the menfolk involved. Later they all put summonses in against each other. The mayor said they were a disgrace to the neighbourhood, and sent Gamble to prison for seven days with hard labour, plus costs of 15s 6d, fined Mrs. Dixon 15 shillings, and dismissed the case against Mr. Dixon. In 1863 a case was brought before the petty sessions involving Mrs. Jane Overfield, and her neighbour Mrs. Sarah Belton, of Brigham's Yard, Butcher Row. As reported in the *Beverley Guardian*:

> *The assault arose out of a sweeping match which took place between the two matrons about noon, immediately after divine service. Mrs. Belton, on returning home from church, ascertained from her daughter, who had been cleaning the doorstep, ... that Mrs. Overfield had swept the dirt back again, whereupon Mrs. Belton took up a brush and sent the dirt back to the defendant's door. That act immediately brought out Mrs. Overfield with brush in hand while her husband was reading his Bible. The ladies had a set to of sweeping the dirt against each other till they were nearly out of breath, and their brushes became entangled, when the performances were brought to a conclusion by Mrs. Overfield giving her adversary a topper.*

The magistrates dismissed the case.

Particularly sad cases concern young women concealing the bodies of babies born illegitimately. Mary Ann Milner of Well Place came before the court in 1867 for that offence, and it was stated that she had been convicted at York

Assizes in 1865 for a similar crime. She lived at home with her mother, but another girl, Maria Robson aged 18, was a living-in servant. She concealed the body of the child in her room for three weeks. A doctor, examining the body, said that it had probably died at birth, presumably as a result of the lack of medical care rather than prematurity or weakness. Maria Robson was sent for trial at York Assizes.

Prostitutes congregated around certain Beverley public houses at night, and were usually allowed to ply their trade unless they disturbed the peace in some way. In 1858 Fanny Steel, described as a 'nymph of the pave', was charged with being drunk and disorderly. She was found by the watchman, lying on her back in Lairgate, screaming. She was too intoxicated to walk, and so the constable called another's assistance and she was carried to the lock-up. Another Fanny, surnamed Turner, 'a young lady of no enviable reputation', was found at 7 p.m. in the Black Bull, Lairgate, on the floor fighting with another woman. Constable Bentley, who had been sent to separate them, sent them both home, but was called out again to her later, when he conveyed her in a wheelbarrow to the lock-up.

Beggars, vagrants and other undesirable characters were often found in the streets. Alice Squires, described as 'a wandering minstrel' was sent to prison for 21 days, having been found drunk and behaving indecently in Friar's Lane in February 1867. Ann Harris, a hawker of caps and needlework, was found drunk and incapable at 6 p.m. in Toll Gavel in March 1867. She denied that she was often so, and was fined five shillings, though it was only to be paid if she was charged again. In the same month Robert Beck, 'a young and trampish apprentice', was found sleeping in the open near the Yorkshire Bank. He said he had applied to enter the workhouse but had been refused because he was not from the Union. He was imprisoned for 21 days. Maria Bean, aged 10, was charged with destitution, having been found at 2.30 a.m. sleeping in a shed in Hind's Yard, Keldgate. She said that she had no parents and had come from Hull looking for work. The Bench discharged her on the understanding that she would leave the town, presumably washing their hands of the problem.

Many of the cases brought before the Bench concerned stealing — of money, food, clothes, animals, and other goods. William Anderson, aged 12, was found guilty in 1858 of stealing £8 16s from the turnkey of the House of Correction, and was sent to reformatory school for five years. In 1867 Samuel Conder, a labourer, was charged with stealing a pair of stockings hung out to dry. The policeman asked him to draw up his trousers, and claimed that he was wearing the stolen goods, but he was acquitted because he persuaded the magistrate that he had bought them. Catherine Green, aged 57, stole a pair of boots in 1868. She pleaded guilty to two other convictions and was sent for seven years penal servitude. Young boys figure quite often in the court reports: William Smith, aged 10 years, was sentenced to three days in prison and six strokes of the birch for stealing two pipes from a tobacconist in Old Waste in 1868.

Beverley had several murders in the mid-Victorian period. In 1857 the *Beverley Guardian* reported a murder and subsequent suicide in the Registrar,

21   Treadmill. (Gloucester Prison).

John Maister's, house in Register Square. Helen Hatfield, a house maid aged 31, had, according to witnesses, been the 'sweetheart' of the gardener, Henry Baker, who was a widower with three children. He asked her to marry him but she refused, giving as her excuse that she wanted Baker's nephew to complete his apprenticeship at the foundry first. Baker was described as a passionate and jealous man, who said that he would hang himself in the greenhouse if she persisted in refusing him. Helen disappeared and eventually her body was discovered at midnight in the garden 'in a bed of artichokes, under an apple tree'. Baker, with his throat cut, was found nearby. He died of his injuries after 12 days. Since he had taken his own life he could not be buried in consecrated ground, and accordingly at midnight:

> *the remains of the wretched man were interred without funeral service, in the midst of a numerous assemblage of spectators, the only light being from a few candles and watchmen's lanterns, and from the dense fog which prevailed at the time the scene was gloomy indeed and seemed to correspond to the melancholy tragedy.*

Riotous behaviour on a minor scale was not unknown in Beverley. The East Yorkshire Militia made a regular visit to the town and exercised on Westwood. The innkeepers regarded their coming with mixed feelings: on the one hand they welcomed the increased business, but on the other hand militiamen tended to be rather high-spirited and disruptive. In May 1862 a private in the Militia was charged with his wife with creating a disturbance in the Garibaldi Inn in

71

Flemingate, where they were lodging. They were said to have 'fought like tigers, and the floor of their chamber was smeared with blood'. The superintendent was called in to arrest them, but a crowd of militiamen gathered to try to prevent it. The superintendent called for reinforcements, and the pair were taken to the Guildhall, where they were put in the lock-up. Thirty to forty militiamen pelted the Guildhall with stones, which were lying in the road to be used for mending it. They splintered the notice board, dented the doors, and broke several windows. The superintendent was injured by a stone. The original offenders and several others were sentenced to two months in gaol, as well as being turned out of the regiment.

A riot which occurred in September 1861 was unique. The occasion was the ending of a 99-year lease on Fishwick's mill, which was situated on the edge of Westwood, on land which the freemen considered to be part of the commons (fig. 20). When the lease expired the freemen decided to reclaim what they considered was part of Westwood, and thus their own property. John Duffill, who was then acting bellman, went round the town with his bell and announced that a meeting of the freemen would take place on Westwood that evening, at 7 o'clock. During the day the members of the Corporation Property Committee visited the premises, and bills were posted against the building stating that any persons found trespassing would be prosecuted. Nevertheless at seven, according to the *Beverley Guardian*, 'a large concourse of persons of all ages and both sexes had assembled in front of the premises, which were guarded by a few borough policemen, Sergeant Dunn being stationed at the south gate and Constable Steel at the one facing west'. On being refused admission to the grounds John Duffill sprang over the gate followed by a crowd of freemen. No resistance was offered by the constables as they immediately saw that it would be useless. They therefore took the names of the ring-leaders, and left to report to their superiors.

The mob then pulled the gate down, and proceeded to stake their right to the mound upon which the mill had been built by sitting upon it in rows:

> one above the other, while numerous pipes and lights were
> brought into requisition, the smokers appearing to enjoy the weed
> all the better for having obtained possession of 'their own' in so
> easy a manner. Two or three juveniles, about ten or twelve years
> of age, when asked what business they had there, replied 'We are
> freemen of Beverley and come to take our rights'.

Some people next began to pull down the mill-house and destroy the fruit trees and shrubberies, as well as sawing down the hedge. About eight o'clock the house was set on fire by putting lighted straw under the staircase, and soon the building, an old one, together with the cart shed adjoining it, were in flames. The fire was visible from a considerable distance and more people came from the town to view the scene and join in the fun despite a heavy downpour of rain. A large haystack was almost set on fire, but it was saved by a few people brushing off the sparks as they fell, and saturating the sides of the rick with water from a nearby pool. The rioters next tried to set fire to the hedge, which was wet with the rain. They brought pieces of wood, and placed it under the hedge to help the flames. Somewhat surprisingly no-one was seriously injured: a few people being treated for superficial wounds and glass in eyes.

The following day sightseers visited the ruins; nothing remained standing but parts of the walls. The hedge was partially burnt down, but remained as a challenge to the rioters, who returned in the evening, pulled down the remaining walls, and renewed their efforts to burn down the hedge. That again put the rick in danger, but its owner, with a body of police, arrived at the scene and succeeded in putting out the fire. The mob threw pieces of turf at them whilst they did so. A criminal trial followed but most of the accused were acquitted. To general satisfaction the land on which the mill had stood reverted to being part of Westwood.

At certain times of the year the Beverley constabulary might be expected to be particularly busy. November 5th marking the anniversary of the uncovering of the Gunpowder Plot was often the occasion for rowdy behaviour. In 1856 a somewhat premature (November 1st) and unofficial bonfire took place in Market Place. Youths burnt tar barrels, rolled them about, and threw fireballs into the shops. Also early in November the town was full for the statute hirings, when the farm servants for miles around changed their employers. The hirings took place in the market towns of the East Riding at a time when the farming year was at its slackest. Hirings week was a time of festivity for the young people who worked hard for the rest of the year. It was also a time when the normal rules of behaviour might be forgotten and policing the town a harder task than it was normally. However, newspaper reports suggest that the young people behaved well. More trouble seems to have been caused by the showmen at the fair, who, according to an account of 1862, displayed considerable ill-will and abuse towards each other. Another report tells how the police were kept busy dealing with 'the light-fingered gentry', who attended the sittings in order to pursue 'their nefarious avocation', but owing to the vigilance of the force 'a great number of rustics were prevented from losing their money'.

Elections were a time when the police were called upon for extra duties. At that time Beverley was bustling with interest and activity and publicans and inn-keepers did excellent business. According to Inspector Holden's account the 1857 election passed off comparatively peacefully, with '... only a few fire balls and a tar barrel'. He gave instructions to the constables not to interfere in any way 'unless danger was likely to ensue to persons or property'. A councillor congratulated Holden on the success of his policy, and said that 'No town in England has experienced greater excitement than Beverley at the late election, yet it passed over without bloodshed, the only damage being a few old pokers and broken chairs thrown about'.

Beverley races took place in June and attracted people from far afield. In general they seem to have been very good-tempered affairs, with little disruption, although cases such as that of a Nottingham man, charged with 'sharp practice', by duping a country lad with the three-card trick on his way to the races in 1868 did appear in the courts. The man received a sentence of one month's hard labour.

Some parts of Beverley were rather less law-abiding than others. Although the town had a reputation for elegance and presented a very attractive appearance to the visitor, it also had its seamy side: side streets and alley ways such as Sylvester Lane figured regularly in criminal reports. Being situated off Saturday Market Place and Ladygate, where there were numerous public houses and inns in mid-century, and being somewhat dark and secluded, Sylvester Lane attracted many undesirables. A report of 1858 stated that when the public houses closed on a Saturday night people congregated in Sylvester Lane, used 'bad and disgusting language', and ignored the watchman on duty when he ordered them to go home. In 1868, two residents, Elizabeth Hobson and Mary Coupland, were charged with riotous and disorderly conduct and shameful language, 'one trying to outdo the other'. They were ordered to keep the peace for six months under a surety of £5, otherwise they would be sent to prison.

Beverley had its problems with delinquents: apparently in 1856 some people, particularly on a Sunday, passed the time together sitting on projecting window ledges in Wednesday Market Place, stretching their legs across the pavement, 'so that respectable people had not only to get off the flagging to pass them, but often got insulted'. Graffiti is not only a modern problem: the same newspaper report mentions house owners having to clean their shutters and walls 'and thus erase the obscene language and figures which [some people's] depraved minds induced them to scribble.

People sentenced to imprisonment, whether at the petty sessions or the quarter sessions, were sent to the House of Correction, which was situated behind the Sessions House, in what is now Norfolk Street, where some of the buildings still remain, having been converted into private houses. It had been opened in 1810, and at that time there were 22 cells in the prison. It was an attractive building, fronted in white brick, with a house for the governor alongside. A wall surrounded the buildings, which a contemporary described as looking from a distance like 'a noble mansion with its domestic offices'. The perception of its inmates may have been rather different. In the mid-Victorian period there were sometimes as many as 100 convicts in the prison at one time. The report of January 1863 stated that for the previous quarter there had been an average of 84 persons in the House of Correction, compared with 80 a year before. Inmates were divided into 14 classes: women were separated from men; convicted people from those on remand; vagrants were housed separately. Separate day-rooms were provided for the various classes.

On admission prisoners were given a bath, and if verminous or dirty, a haircut. They were supplied with the regulation prison dress, and thereafter with a weekly change of linen. Prisoners in the House of Correction were strictly segregated, especially after 1835 when the so-called 'Silent System' was instituted. That was intended not only to punish, but also to prevent the corruption of first offenders by contact with more hardened prisoners. The diet was very basic, meat being given only on certain days with oatmeal and bread forming the main constituents. Convicted prisoners serving less than a week received no meat at all. Religious instruction, presumably in the hope of reformation, formed an important part of the prison routine. Prayers were read regularly by the prison chaplain. Inmates were supplied with a Bible, and other improving literature. A schoolmaster attended to teach the younger inmates.

The prisoners were expected to work, at hard physical tasks, such as picking oakum, breaking stones, building work, and so on. But, many people were sentenced to hard labour, which meant working the treadmill. The treadmill, or tread-wheel, was the invention of William Cubitt in 1817. It was introduced into many prisons, including Beverley, in the first half of the 19th century. Beverley's most famous prisoner, the Chartist, Robert Peddie, has left a vivid description of working the treadmill in the House of Correction in the 1840s. It was housed in a building (still standing and now an attractive house) in the centre of the prison complex. The building was open on one side, so that the prisoners were visible from the road, and 'daily exposed to gratify the idle curiosity of spectators, like wild beasts in a menagerie'.

The wheel was actually a cylinder with steps around its outer circumference like the wheel of a paddle steamer. Each prisoner was divided from his neighbour by a wooden screen (fig. 21). He had a rail or ledge to grip in order to prevent him from falling forward. The wheel went round inexorably, and its resistance could be regulated by a governor. Prisoners were made to work the wheel for spells of twenty minutes at a time. After a rest of ten minutes they resumed and carried on until they had completed the stipulated labour of 'ascent', which varied from one prisoner to another. At the time of Peddie's incarceration the maximum height was 12,000 feet daily for men, and 10,000 for women. In 1859 the regulations were modified so that no female prisoner or boy under 14 was to work the mill. Peddie described the effects of working the treadmill as including hot sweats, headaches, nausea, vomiting, and giddiness. Undoubtedly it was a harsh punishment, hardly alleviated by the fact that those who worked the mill received a slightly better diet (meat daily) than those who did not. In some prisons the wheel had no function other than to provide labour for the prisoners, but in Beverley the wheel produced whiting from chalk.

Harsh punishments such as the treadmill were acceptable to a government that was becoming more and more concerned about what it believed to be an increase in crime. Partly that increase may have been the result of more efficient policing, partly it may have resulted from a greater willingness to prosecute supported by society's higher expectations of public behaviour. However, the increase was more apparent in the growing industrial cities. Small country towns such as Beverley were probably as law-abiding in mid-century, if not more so, than they had been fifty to a hundred years earlier.

CHAPTER FIVE
THE TREATMENT OF THE POOR

Beverley was a relatively flourishing place in the mid-Victorian period, and work was available for most people who required it. But there were always those who for various reasons could not support themselves and who were therefore dependent on private charity or the poor rates. Such people included the temporarily sick, the insane, the crippled, widows, orphans, deserted wives, unmarried mothers, and perhaps the largest category of all, the aged. Old people had to work until they were no longer able, and then were forced to rely on help from relations if it were available, otherwise private charity or parish relief was often their only support. Private charity was dispensed by almshouses and welfare trusts established by the bequests of individual philanthropists, for example a 'Lying-In Charity' for pregnant women helped them with the expenses of childbirth. In addition, people sometimes made provision for illness and funeral expenses by joining friendly societies. Poor relief was provided by a rate levied on property value and was dispensed in the form of either 'outdoor relief' or 'indoor relief'. Outdoor relief consisted in the payment of a regular cash allowance to the pauper living at home, or in the provision of occasional allowances of fuel, clothing and food. Indoor relief was that given to the pauper residing in a workhouse.

The town was well-supplied with almshouses and charitable trusts. Persons who had led blameless lives (described in a contemporary guide as 'poor old deserving individuals'), and who could obtain a recommendation from the relevant trustees, might be fortunate in obtaining accommodation in one of those institutions. Most of them were intended for women only. Fox's Hospital in Minster Moorgate housed four women 'of good character' who had been resident in Beverley for at least twenty years. As well as accommodation they received 13s 8d monthly, a gown every two years, and a chaldron (about 25 hundredweight) of coal once a year. Ann Routh's Hospital in Keldgate had been established in 1749, also for poor women. By the mid-19th century 32 widows were living there, in separate rooms, and provided with five shillings each weekly. Three of them were paid extra for acting as matron and resident nurses. In Minster Moorgate stood Charles Warton's Hospital, for poor widows, who had to be aged 60 years or over. They received four shillings each weekly, and an allowance of coal. Nearby stood Sir Michael Warton's Hospital which had room for another six aged widows. The Corporation almshouses housed 27 people in the bede houses — four cottages in Lairgate —which were rebuilt in 1862, and in the maison dieu, comprising 14 rooms, at the southern end of Lairgate (rebuilt in Morton Lane in 1934). Tymperon House (fig. 22), in Walkergate, housed six men and women (two of whom had to be from the parish of Aldborough) who were provided with six shillings weekly.

There were many other smaller charitable trusts, often used to provide coal, bread, or extra food at Christmas. Money gifts were also provided by some charities, though according to Green's guide to the town, published in 1847, money could be made 'to serve other and far different wants from those contemplated by the donors'. Some charities were established for particular purposes: Matthew Turner, in his will proved in 1856, established a fund (still extant) from which female domestic servants living within eight miles of the Guildhall could receive single payments of ten guineas for good service, on recommendation from their employers.

Before the provision of old age pensions and sickness benefit people were expected to make their own arrangements to support themselves during periods of illness and when they became too old to work. Some joined friendly societies, which for a relatively modest outlay of a few pence per week provided a modicum of support when a member was sick. A 'funeral benefit' was also paid on the death of the member and his wife. Beverley had several friendly societies in the mid-19th century; they included the Ancient Order of Foresters, which had three courts in Beverley, the largest having 226 members in 1865, and three lodges of the Independent Order of Oddfellows (Manchester Unity), with a total of 569 members in 1862.

From 1836, after the passage of the Poor Law Amendment Act in 1834, Beverley was the centre of a Poor Law Union which included 32 villages and hamlets around the town. Prior to that date relief had been organised on a parish level, with each community looking after its own poor. The aim of the new Act was to decrease the burden of the poor rates by taking all paupers into a centrally situated workhouse. It was assumed that a number of those receiving relief would cease to apply when they realised that they would be compelled to enter an institution. Guardians of the Poor were appointed for each parish as administrators.

In 1836, when the Beverley Union was formed, there was already a workhouse in Beverley. It was situated in Minster Moorgate (fig. 23) and had been built in 1727 to cater for 100 paupers. Despite its age it was considered suitable for adaption to the new system. Carpenters, glaziers, bricklayers, and plasterers, were set to work to alter it internally and externally. New sheds were built, perimeter walls of nine feet high were renewed or rebuilt, and iron bars were fitted to several windows. The workhouse had been designed in the form of a letter H, with the central section containing the master's quarters, and the kitchen and larder behind. The womens' and girls' wards were well separated from those for men and boys. There was a lying-in ward (for unmarried mothers) and sick wards.

By the 1850s the workhouse was being criticised for its lack of facilities. A Poor Law inspector reported in 1858 that there was insufficient room available and that vagrants' wards were needed, that the infection wards were unsatisfactory, and that the roof needed repair; he concluded that a new workhouse should be built. Since taking over the workhouse in 1836 the Guardians had spent over £1,200 on repairs, but more were required. However at a meeting of the Board of Guardians vehement opposition to the building of a new workhouse was led by Daniel Boyes, who stated that if they were to decide on a new building it would no doubt be in a costly style, new staff such as porters, schoolmasters and mistresses would be required, and that new inspectors always felt the need to recommend 'something new and absurd'. A committee was set up to report on the matter, and it recommended the adaptation of the present workhouse with the erection of a female vagrants' ward and alterations to convert the 'dead house' (mortuary) and the 'chip house' (presumably carpentry shop) into a vagrants' ward for men. New buildings to house the mortuary, the chip house and a saw pit were to be constructed in the garden. The following year the Board was considering purchasing some land adjoining the workhouse in order to extend it. The Poor Law inspector pointed out that those improvements would only be satisfactory for a few years and that it would be preferable to obtain a new site with space for the growing of vegetables. It was suggested that the land and a building large enough for 150 people would cost no more than £3,500.

The inspector's arguments seem to have prevailed, for in October 1858 it was agreed that a new workhouse should be constructed at a cost of not more than £2,600, and a site was selected on a field belonging to the Society of Friends at the top of Wood Lane. That was bought in 1860 together with one adjoining, and enthusiasm for the new project began to grow, the Guardians deciding that the new building should be a credit to Beverley even if it meant exceeding the original estimate.

The site selected was a most attractive one, overlooking Westwood. The new workhouse, designed by J. B. and W. Atkinson of York, in the Tudor style, still remains today, forming the core of Westwood Hospital. It is a handsome building (fig. 24), with careful attention to detail, exemplified by the beaver crests above the entrances. A new road was made from the town, originally named Union Road, but later changed to Woodlands. The architect inspected the finished building in March 1861, and pronounced himself very satisfied with the builder's work — there was 'neither flinch, flaw nor crack' anywhere. The extra land purchased seems to have been regarded as a liability: in March 1863 Daniel Boyes claimed that 'it demoralised the paupers' because when they were allowed onto it they tended to 'escape' into the town. Another Guardian suggested that the land was needed for the cultivation of vegetables to put in the paupers' soup, but shortly after that discussion it was sold.

It is apparent from the minutes of Guardians' meetings that when the New Poor Law was implemented in Beverley the intention was to take everyone into the workhouse as soon as practicable. In 1837 it was minuted that it would be necessary for a time to provide relief to non-residents, but that they must attend the Receiving Officer to gain his permission. In May of that year it was decided (by a vote of 12 to 9) that unmarried mothers who had 'borne only one bastard child and have been previously and subsequently women of good conduct' should be granted outdoor relief. In January 1839 a motion was put by James Mould Robinson that from the end of the month 'all outdoor relief to able-bodied paupers be discontinued'. However Daniel Boyes suggested that a decision should be postponed until the 29th February. That was agreed to by a majority of 21 to 5. Perhaps some of those agreeing had forgotten that such a date only occurred in a leap year, which meant that discussion was postponed for over a year! The minutes for meetings between mid-1839 and 1867 have been lost so that the decision taken in 1840 remains unknown, but it is apparent that outdoor relief continued for a majority of paupers. For example on May 24th 1856 the weekly statement shows that there were in the workhouse that week 33 adults described as not able-bodied, 14 able-bodied adults, and 30 children. The outdoor poor consisted of 414 adults described as not able-bodied, 53 able-bodied, and 165 children. Clearly the New Poor Law was not being implemented in Beverley as it had been intended by its founders in 1834.

A 19th-century workhouse combined the functions of old people's home, orphanage, mental asylum, hospital, and refuge for unmarried mothers. That is well-demonstrated by looking at the census returns for 1851. On the night of 30th March 1851 there were 67 inmates in Beverley workhouse. Almost half of them (32) were children, eight of whom were in the workhouse without their parents, either because they were orphaned or deserted. The remainder were with their mothers, of whom eight were unmarried, and five were widowed or deserted by their husbands. There were eight men and three women over 60 in the workhouse. The other residents were six men aged between 23 and 47, five women aged between 23 and 25, and one woman aged 56. All but one of the women (a washerwoman) were former servants, whilst the men were all former labourers, except for a butcher and a bleacher.

People described as 'idiots', 'deranged', 'demented', or 'partially insane' were commonly kept in the workhouse, hardly suitable companions for the children. In 1867 the workhouse master reported that there were eight 'imbeciles' in the house, who needed watching but did not require restraint. Until the establishment of the mental asylum at Walkington in 1865 the alternatives would have been to have sent them to the Hull Borough Asylum, to the North and East Riding Asylum at York, or to one of the many private asylums.

The workhouse also gave temporary shelter to vagrants who had a right to apply to the workhouse master for one night's lodging. In the old workhouse vagrants' wards were situated at some distance from the principal building, which meant that they could not be properly supervised. In the new workhouse the vagrants' wards were closer to the main house. The conditions provided do not seem to have been very welcoming; a Cambridgeshire tramp told Beverley magistrates in 1865 that he had run away from the workhouse because it was cold and infested with vermin. On going into the vagrants' ward he had seen some writing on the wall to the effect that 'there's nothing here but hunger and cold, nothing to eat and you will have nothing but lice and bugs'. He examined the rugs, and found them 'in an animated state'. Nevertheless the wards continued to be used. In 1866 an increase in the numbers of vagrants was causing concern: an average of 15 were accommodated nightly. Those who requested supper were required to break stones the following morning, but were leaving without accomplishing that task. The Guardians decided that breakfast should be withheld until the work was done. Apparently in Driffield and other unions no supper was provided, and vagrants were coming to Beverley in preference. In 1866 the Guardians decided that supper should be discontinued, and that labour for four hours would be required for a night's lodging. A policeman supervised the vagrants while they worked. In 1868 an inspector's report said that the tramps should be provided with better bedding

*22   Tymperon House. Luke Clennell, c.1835. (East Yorkshire Borough of Beverley
Borough Council).*

*23   Workhouse, Minster Moorgate. Luke Clennell, c.1835. (East Yorkshire Borough of Beverley
Borough Council).*

— clean straw and rugs.

The staff required for a workhouse was usually quite small, since the inmates themselves were able to undertake the domestic duties. In 1836 the Board of Guardians decided that they would appoint a master at £50 per annum, with his wife as matron at £20 per annum. John and Fanny Wilkinson of Hull were chosen for the duties. The workhouse master and mistress held positions of particular power and responsibility, and in Beverley the people who put themselves forward were not always the most suitable. In 1844 John Wilkinson was the subject of a paternity charge, though he survived as master until the 1850s, when he was replaced by John Hudson. In 1864 a nurse at the workhouse accused Hudson of allowing members of his family to come and go 'at all hours' and of supplying them with meals (including ham and coffee) from the workhouse kitchens. At that time Hudson was not dismissed, but was asked to restrict family visits, and it was the nurse who resigned. It was decided not to replace her, there being few sick persons in the house, and an inmate fulfilled the duties of nurse. In 1867 Hudson himself resigned, having been accused of interfering with the young girls in the house. The Guardians appointed James and Elizabeth Shives as master and matron, and a few months later a nurse-cum-assistant matron was appointed. The Shives were unable to run the workhouse efficiently and were judged incompetent after a few months and asked to resign. In September 1868 Mr. and Mrs. Dawe were appointed in their place.

Other staff employed included a porter, but in the old workhouse one was employed only irregularly, the duties apparently being relatively light, and the building easy to superintend. In the new workhouse, which was far larger and did not have a high wall around it, the paupers were difficult to oversee. In 1867 Daniel Boyes suggested that a wall should be put around the building and a porter's lodge built. He said that he had seen a woman leaving the workhouse looking 'uncommonly stout', and the chances were that she was 'as laden as a honey bee' with stolen goods. The inmates came and went at will, and an old man had been caught in the garden throwing vegetables to someone outside. The following year when the matter came up again Boyes said that:

> when poor old Mr. Wilkinson was in charge of the old workhouse he could keep all in, and find time in the bargain to take the children out and let them sing a hymn in the streets ... the old workhouse was more compact ... the present workhouse was too big for the purpose and the inmates were so scattered about there was no knowing where to find them.

Particular attention was paid to the spiritual needs of inmates, and it became the practice to appoint a workhouse chaplain. In some workhouses a school was provided, but in Beverley the children went to nearby local schools. In 1862 the Poor Law inspector recommended that a schoolmistress should be appointed to teach the children inside the workhouse, but the Guardians decided that it was preferable for the children to go out and mix with others so that they should not become pauperised when young. In 1866 the matter again

81

came up: the inspector said that the children were sent to three different schools, often without anyone to take them and keep them out of mischief on their journey. If there were a school in the workhouse the girls could also make and repair their own clothes, thus saving money, and the schoolmistress's salary would be paid by a government grant. The Board again turned down the suggestion.

When the Minster Moorgate workhouse became the Union workhouse its furniture and fittings were considered inadequate. One hundred iron bedsteads were immediately ordered, together with the necessary bedding and chaff mattresses. A Beverley ironmonger supplied a 'full-sized tin bath, a large bell, 6 rice pudding tins, 4 candlesticks at 4/- each, two fire-guards and one iron boiler to hold 3½ gallons'. Another shopkeeper supplied a deal table, a trencher rack to hold 100 trenchers (for bread), two tin racks to hold 200 tins (presumably for the paupers to eat from), 205 feet of pine racks for the kitchen, five towel rollers, a meat tray, and 'two childrens' stools with tins for same'. Three dozen horn spoons were bought for the children (adults may have been expected to eat with their fingers as was certainly the case elsewhere), a bench 'with a back' was supplied for the old men to sit on, blinds were bought for the sickroom window, and two new fireplaces were put in at a cost of £12 10s.

In both the old and new workhouses the sexes were segregated at night. The wards were sparsely furnished with iron bedsteads and chaff mattresses. Personal hygiene must have been a problem: people were washed and disinfected when they first came into the workhouse but how frequently they bathed thereafter is not known. In the old workhouse the only bath-house was situated some distance from the main building at the bottom of the yard. In the new workhouse the washing facilities in the wards were also inadequate, judging from a medical officer's report in 1868. He said that hair brushes should be provided for the boys and girls, and wash basins, towels and drinking vessels should be placed in all the wards. Apparently in some wards only one towel per week and one comb and brush were provided for all to share.

When paupers entered the workhouse they were provided with clothing by the Guardians. In the 1830s the accounts show that the women and girls were supplied with green and white straw bonnets at 13s 6d and 11s 6d per dozen respectively, whilst the men and boys wore 'Scotch caps'. Large quantities of various types of cloth, for example, grey calico, brown harden, fustian, lindsey woolsey and checked muslin, were supplied by a local draper, and a dressmaker was employed, with the help of the inmates, to make the clothing. Shoes were supplied at prices ranging from 7s 6d per pair for men to 3s 3d for girls aged 6 to 12. In 1862 the clothing required by the workhouse for one year included mens' and boys' ready-made coats, waistcoats and trousers, mens' breeches, mens' and boys' hats and caps, shoes for men, women and children, and strong 'ancle' boots for boys. Blankets for single and double beds, bed rugs, cotton sheeting, handkerchiefs, womens' and girls' bonnets and stays, materials for making clothing, comprising cotton shirting, flannel, prints, chambrey, harden, Brown Holland, worsted, thread, and tape were also listed.

The uniformity of dress must have been a constant reminder to the paupers that they were the recipients of charity. On Sundays they were all required to attend church or chapel, and the children went out daily to school. In 1865 the master applied to the Guardians for capes to be supplied for the boys to wear in wet weather. In 1868 all the workhouse girls were brought into the Guardians' meeting to 'show off their new clothes' — somewhat surprisingly these were alpaca frocks and capes and hats trimmed with green velvet. As reported in the *Beverley Guardian*, 'The little things curtseyed to the Guardians and said that they had come to thank them for their new clothes ... The girls, the youngest of whom was scarcely able to toddle, then left the room, evidently much pleased with their new habiliments'.

Because life in the workhouse was designed to be 'less eligible', that is somewhat worse, than life outside, the food supplied to the paupers was very basic. The diet used in Beverley workhouse was one of those recommended by the Poor Law Commissioners as follows:

Day	Breakfast	Dinner	Supper
Sunday) Tuesday)- Thursday)	-((Men: 6oz. bread, 1½ pts. gruel (Women: 5oz. bread 1½ pts. gruel	5oz. meat, 8oz. potatoes 5oz. meat 8oz. potatoes	6oz. bread 1½ pts. gruel 5oz. bread 1½ pts. gruel
Monday) Wednesday)- Saturday)	-((Men: as above (Women: as above	1½ pts. soup 1½ pts. soup	6oz. bread 2oz. cheese 5oz. bread 2oz. cheese
Friday	-((Men: as above (Women: as above	14oz. suet pudding or rice pudding as above	6oz. bread 1½ pts. gruel as above

Shortly after adopting that diet in 1837 the Guardians decided to modify it: bread was served at dinner on Monday, Wednesday, and Saturday, a small quantity of pease was added to the soup on those days and treacle sauce was served with the suet pudding on Fridays. However the cheese and bread which had been served for supper on Mondays, Wednesdays and Saturdays were replaced by gruel. Those modifications, it was said, would not add to the expense, but would 'contribute greatly to the comfort of the paupers'.

The meals were supposed to be measured out carefully so that everyone received their entitlement. Mr. Shives complained in 1867 that when preparing breakfast for 70-80 people he had to cut up and weigh every piece of bread. Inmates criticised its quality from time to time. In 1856 it was reported to be badly baked and unfit to eat. There was no cook and the master and matron, with help from the female inmates, prepared the food. When Mr. and Mrs. Shives began work in 1867 they complained that the workhouse was completely disorganised: the meal-times were irregular, and instead of eating in the dining room people were taking their meals all over the house. Tins, spoons and knives were taken away from the kitchen and lost. However the Shives do not seem to have succeeded in bringing order since on one Sunday in February 1869 a medical officer visited the workhouse and found that the master, matron and nurse had gone for a walk, and the inmates of the sick ward were 'feasting on black pudding and tea' (though it was explained later that black puddings were sent in to some patients in the sick and lying-in wards on Saturdays). A few days earlier it was reported that during some horse-play in the workhouse a galosh had been put in some gruel. When asked about that incident Mr. Shives said that the gruel had not been spoiled; he had tasted it himself.

In 1862, when there were about 80 people living in the workhouse, the provisions required were as follows:

Provisions for three months:

Flour — best seconds wheaten flour (2s 1½d per stone)	470	stones
Beef without bone: buttock, mouse buttock, thick flank,		
neck, or sticking piece (supplied at 4s 11d per lb.)	140	stones
Mutton: necks and loins (5d per lb.)	10	stones
Suet (5d per lb.)	40	lbs.
Beasts' heads (1s 8½d each)	40	

Groceries for 6 months:

Good black tea (4s per lb.)	40	lbs.
Good coffee (1s per lb.)	4	lbs.
Raw sugar (6s per stone)	26	stones
Brown soap (4s 6d per stone)	40	stones
Oatmeal	80	stones
Salt	36	stones
Treacle	6	stones
Rice	10	stones
Soda	12	stones
Fresh butter	200	lbs.
White pepper	6	lbs.
Starch	24	lbs.
Powder blue	3	lbs.
Sago	112	lbs.
Peas	no	amnt.
Dip candles	no	amnt.

The list does not include potatoes, which must have been either grown in the gardens or supplied weekly. All workhouse diets seem to have been deficient in green vegetables, though they too may have been grown. Mr. Shives said in 1868 that when potatoes were in short supply he gave vegetables such as cabbage in their place. Fruit never appeared in any form. Milk was supplied by a local cowkeeper. Tea was supplied to the elderly only. In 1863 the average cost of maintaining a pauper in Beverley workhouse was said to be 2s 7½d per week.

The normal daily routine was quite rigid. After breakfast the paupers separated to their various tasks and duties: the children set out for school, usually in the charge of an adult pauper. The women were assigned to domestic

24   *New workhouse (now Westwood Hospital). (Humberside Arts and Leisure).*

THE YORKSHIRE CLOTHES WASHING MACHINE,

B Y which a direct saving of at least FIFTY PER CENT. is effected, and washing rendered a comparatively pleasant affair

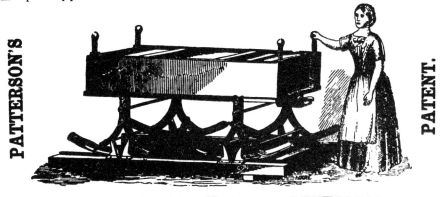

JOHN PATTERSON & Co., BEVERLEY,

Are now manufacturing this newly-invented Washing Machine, which in every desirable point far surpasses anything that has been hitherto offered to the public for this purpose.

Price of Ordinary Size   -   -   £3. 10s. net Cash.

To enable those who may be wishful to satisfy themselves respecting the utility of these Machines to do so without purchasing in the first instance, they will be lent out if required, free of charge, for the space of two weeks, simply on condition that they are returned, carriage paid and unbroken, if not approved of.

25   *Washing machine advertisement.* **Beverley Guardian**. *(Humberside Arts and Leisure).*

duties, cleaning, preparing food, cooking, sewing, and washing. There were large drying yards in the old workhouse which were also used by the women as exercise yards, and there were drying rooms for wet weather. In 1867 a washing machine was bought for the house. That may have been the one which was being advertised in the *Beverley Guardian* at the time (fig. 25).

The able-bodied men were expected to work outside, breaking up cobbles for the road, or picking oakum (unravelling tarry ropes for caulking ships). In 1861 the suggestion was made that able-bodied paupers should be employed as street-sweepers. That was agreed to and the corporation paid the Guardians one shilling per day for their services. White smocks were to be provided as they 'would look cleaner than fustian and wash easily'.

The sick paupers were cared for in separate wards, nursed mainly by other inmates. Male inmates received a tobacco allowance if they worked on the sick wards. Medical officers were appointed to visit the sick regularly. From 1865 medicines given to the sick poor included cod liver oil and quinine. Two reports in 1868 were very critical of the equipment in the sick wards: there were no mats on the floors, the beds were chaff when they should be flock or hair, there were no dressing gowns for people sitting up in bed, and the fever wards were too close to the old mens' and womens' yards. Those matters were rectified by 1869.

The women in the lying-in wards were also cared for by inmates and visiting doctors. In 1868 a Poor Law inspector suggested that milk bottles should be supplied for the babies, that pictures of a suitably religious nature should be put on the walls, and that the nursing mothers should be provided with rocking chairs. Coconut-fibre matting was also needed for the infants to crawl and walk on in the young womens' day room. Those suggestions incensed the frugal Daniel Boyes, who said that he had brought up a large family and 'never had a rocking chair or cradle in his house in his life'.

The old men and old women also worked on light tasks if they were able, and seem to have been well-treated on the whole. In 1866 two seats were placed outside for the old women to sit on, and presumably look over Westwood. Their diet was more varied and they were allowed to leave the workhouse more often than were the younger inmates. In 1867 they were allowed to go into town daily. However the master stated that they had not been returning at regular times and asked that their privilege be withdrawn. They were only to be allowed out on Mondays, Thursdays, and Sundays. The other paupers were officially allowed out on Sundays only, but when the workhouse was being inefficiently run in 1867 and 1868 everyone seems to have been coming and going at will. It even appears that some people were living in the workhouse and going out into the town to work. From September 1868 that practice was only allowed with special permission from the Guardians.

Punishments for even minor misdemeanours could be severe. In 1857 Sarah Ann Beck was placed in solitary confinement for eight hours for refusing to work. She said that she preferred prison to the workhouse and was taken before the magistrates. One old man was confined to the workhouse for a month owing to his having set fire to his bed-clothes when lighting his pipe. Deprivation of food was another punishment applied. The children seem to have been quite disruptive at times: in 1867 the matron complained that the girls were very disobedient 'owing to the want of some proper person to take charge of them when not at school. The best person there is in the house to mind them fights the children and they fight her in return and use most disgusting language one towards the other'. When the children were not at school they seem to have had few means of amusing themselves. The inspector's report in 1868 suggested that toys should be provided, but whether they were is not clear. At that time there were some pets in the workhouse: in February 1868 the subject of the presence of cats and dogs in the house came up for discussion when it was revealed that one of the cats belonged to a female pauper. Daniel Boyes said he had never heard tell of such a thing as a pauper keeping a cat. It was decided that it should not be allowed in the future.

Death in the workhouse was commonplace. Coffins were made in the carpentry shop on the premises by the paupers themselves. The inmates seem to have been very reluctant to act as bearers, and in 1866 a 'hand carriage' was hired at a cost of 2s 6d per funeral. The Guardians considered buying a carriage, but decided against it. They did however purchase some black material to cover the coffin.

Because of the high proportion of children, life in Beverley workhouse may have been quite noisy and even lively. Many of the young women were rather volatile, and fights between them were relatively common. When the Shives were running the workhouse in 1867-8 the routine seems to have been completely disrupted. With a competent person in charge, the regime must have been very rigidly organised. The Guardians held their meetings monthly, and normally seem to have kept a close watch upon the workhouse. It did not take them long to realise that their appointment of Mr. and Mrs. Shives had been a mistake, although Mr. Hudson's activities with the young girls may have been carried on for a long time without detection. The Guardians' first duty, as they saw it, was to run the system with as little charge as possible on the ratepayers, and life in Beverley workhouse reflected that preoccupation. Most of the improvements that were made in the 1850s and 1860s were made as a result of inspectors' reports, rather than being initiated by the Guardians.

Throughout the 1850s and 1860s the workhouse was never full, and the number of people being provided with outdoor relief always exceeded the number inside the house. The amount of assistance varied according to the needy persons' circumstances: in the 1830s an able-bodied man was given assistance to the value of four shillings per week, together with two shillings for his wife and one shilling and six pence for each child, and those allowances probably remained the same for several decades. The carer of a deserted baby was allowed two shillings and six pence per week in 1856. Relief was normally given in cash, though at certain times flour, clothes, and fuel were distributed. During a cholera outbreak in Beverley in 1866 the medical officers were authorised to supply disinfectants to paupers at risk from the disease. A handbill was circulated warning against drinking impure water. Loans were made to help people over temporary difficulties, or to allow them to become independent: Richard Watson, who was in the workhouse with his wife and four children, was lent £3 in order to buy furniture and set himself up independently.

When the workhouse was in Minster Moorgate the outdoor paupers (or someone acting on their behalf) had to go there to collect their relief. When the new workhouse was built it was considered to be rather far out of the town, and the infants' school in Minster Moorgate was used as a distribution point. At that time there were said to be 300 persons living in Beverley and Woodmansey obtaining relief in that way.

Certain streets in Beverley had more than their fair share of poverty: the 1851 census for Sylvester Lane shows several households of paupers. Most of them were elderly, like Hannah Musgrove, a 66 year-old widow, who lived with her two-year-old grandson. Many old women, and less frequently old men, were taken in by their adult children, and received a few shillings per week for their food. They were probably able to make themselves useful to the household minding children and undertaking light domestic duties.

The continuance of outdoor relief was dependent upon good behaviour. In May 1857 Ellen Knowles's out-relief was discontinued when she was found to be 'keeping a bad house' whilst neglecting her children, who were said to be filthy and diseased. They were all taken into the workhouse. The records show a number of cases of husbands refusing to support their wives. Ann McDougle came before the Guardians in 1866 asking to be taken into the workhouse because her husband would not support her even though he earned 30s per week at the Foundry. Some people seem to have preferred death to the workhouse. In 1863 an old man was found almost dead in a stable in Norwood. He had not eaten for a fortnight and was taken into the workhouse to be given medical attention. He was said to have been an inmate on several occasions but preferred starving to death to going back. In 1865 Beverley made the national news when an old woman from Woodmansey died of starvation. Her daughter told the coroner that her mother managed to support herself in summer with agricultural work, but that when she had applied to the Board of Guardians for outdoor relief in the winter she had been told that she would have to come into the workhouse. That she would not do, saying she would rather starve. Her body was in an emaciated state when found, and there was no food in the house. The coroner said that he felt it rather harsh not to allow her a few shillings in winter, when she maintained herself for the rest of the year. The Guardians' excuse was that she had failed to submit her application at the right time.

Beverley seems to have been fairly typical of the rest of the country (or at least of the northern areas) in the way that the New Poor Law was applied. Most relief was given outside the workhouse, not for humanitarian reasons, but because it was found to be cheaper. Those people within the workhouse were generally cared for adequately by the standards of the day, but the lack of freedom, the segregation, and the monotonous diet, must have made the daily life of the inmates very unappealing. Fortunately they did at least get some respite from their frugal diet at Christmas when a subscription was raised in the town to supply a good dinner and various treats to the inmates. In 1869 the *Beverley Guardian* reported:

> *It will be a matter of satisfaction to those who have been enjoying the festive season in luxury, to know that Christmas is*

not shut out from those whose misfortune it is to seek the shelter of the workhouse. At our own union the fare on Christmas Day was roast beef, legs of mutton, plum pudding, and beer, which the inmates did justice to, and enjoyed most thoroughly. In the afternoon the children were supplied with raisins, nuts, oranges, and treacle cake; the women with four ounces of tea and a two-pound cake each; and the men with a quarter of a pound of tobacco each... On Christmas Eve... the inmates were regaled with a plentiful supply of frumenty.

CHAPTER SIX
RELIGION AND EDUCATION

Religion played an important part in the social and institutional life of Victorian Britain, and Beverley was no exception, with several of its schools established by religious bodies, and many of its social activities centring around church and chapel. The town was strongly Protestant, and at times anti-Catholicism was vehemently expressed. There was a wide variety of denominations in the town, with Methodism, both Wesleyan and Primitive, being particularly well-supported.

In 1851, in connection with the usual ten-yearly census of population, the government decided that a religious census should be taken on Sunday, March 30th. Ministers were asked to provide information upon available accommodation, and to make a head count of everyone attending services on that day. The census was unpopular in some quarters, and was never repeated. It was regarded as an intrusion of privacy, and supporters of the Church of England found it particularly unacceptable, seeing it as an attempt to disestablish their church if it were found that its adherents were not in a majority. The figures of attendance when published were greeted with a mixture of dismay and disbelief. They showed that only about half of the population of England and Wales over ten years old had attended church that day. Many people doubted the veracity of the census, and indeed it may not have presented an accurate picture, since ministers knew the date of the count in advance, and there would be a natural temptation to try to arrange a higher than usual attendance on that day. Moreover most churches and chapels held two or three services on a Sunday, and in view of the rivalry between church and chapel more people than usual may have attended their place of worship twice or more in order to increase the numbers.

The figures for Beverley show that there were over 6,000 individual attendances at church and chapel on census day. 41.2 per cent of those counted went to the Anglican churches, 56.2 per cent to the nonconformist chapels, and 2.6 per cent to the Roman Catholic church. The apparent strength of nonconformism cannot have pleased the clergy of the Minster and St. Mary's, though perhaps it did not surprise them.

Then as now the Minster was the principal architectural ornament of Beverley (frontispiece). It was not however valued by everyone. In 1868 it was said that over the previous few months 1,000 panes of glass had been broken by people throwing stones or using catapults, whilst the stone work and gravestones had been defaced, and the churchyard was used as an 'urchins' playground'. The Minster had been 'Georgianised' in the 18th century by the addition of classical furnishings and accessories, but by the mid-Victorian period most had been removed. The cupola over the central crossing and the classical galleries and pews in the nave were taken down in 1824, though the Grecian-style choir screen remained until 1876, and 'from its incongruity, and

90

total dissimilarity to the rest of the church' it was 'a great eyesore' to the sensitive observer, as was the white and yellow wash which covered the masonry inside. In 1866, as part of the restoration of the church under the direction of Sir Gilbert Scott, the layers of both white and yellow wash were scraped off. From the 1820s the nave was not used by the congregation, the choir and the south small transept being fitted with box pews and galleries, and only a relatively small part of the church being used for services. That remained the seating arrangement until the late 1860s, when the nave was again fitted with pews.

The vicarage was opposite the Minster, on the corner of Eastgate and Minster Yard North. Throughout the period the incumbent was the Reverend, (from 1867, Canon), J. B. Birtwhistle. He and his family were very active in the town and his work in the parish, particularly in connection with the Minster schools, was much praised. When he died in 1879, aged 76, he was described as 'a fearlessly outspoken man ... connected with nearly every good work in the town' and as 'a ready friend to the poor, cheery, kind, who entered sports and pastimes of the children with zest'.

In the mid-19th century, when services were held in the virtually unheated Minster chancel, St. John's Chapel (usually known as the Minster Chapel of Ease) in Lairgate was the place of worship favoured by fashionable folk since it was comfortable and warm. That building, still standing, though a shadow of its former self, is now the Memorial Hall. It was designed by H. F. Lockwood in an Early English style and was opened in 1841 (fig. 26). It had 900 seats, of which 300 were described in 1864 as being free — a reference to the practice of renting pews to individuals. The practice was socially divisive and was going out of favour in the mid-Victorian period. In 1846 a house was erected next to the chapel for the assistant curate from the Minster to occupy.

Beverley's second parish church, St. Mary's, served the northern part of the town. It too underwent refurbishment in the period, much needed if an editorial in the *Beverley Guardian* of 1856 may be believed. Externally the church had been somewhat restored in the early 1850s under the direction of the Pugins, father and son, when the flying buttresses had been added to the south transept, and the turrets on the west front had been rebuilt. The writer of the editorial did not like the flying buttresses, which he described as glaringly obtrusive. But he reserved his strongest words for the interior. He imagined the reactions of a stranger entering the church:

> *Half a door ... will admit him to the transept. The irregular and broken stones, which form the pavement, are dank with perpetual moisture ... the fissured wall appears **not** to support the roof. ... Pews up and pews down – pews facing east and facing west –sinking northward or southward; dark worm-eaten oak, patched with begrimed but unpainted deal - dingy baize hanging in tatters from rusty nails ... a prevailing wash of yellow ... all around pillars and walls are disfigured by the marks left by the removal of the galleries, and the cutting down of the screens and canopies which once protected the worshippers from observation and cold.*

91

At that time the nave was used for services. The cost of the Pugins' work ruled out any further expenditure until the mid-1860s, when a major internal restoration of the church took place under the direction of Sir Gilbert Scott. The old pews were removed and open seats put in their place. An alabaster pulpit replaced the wooden octagonal one, and many memorial stained glass windows were added. The vicarage was in Vicar Lane, opposite the church. The vicar from 1856 to 1873 was the Reverend Boulton Brander. From the early 1860s the Reverend Charles Easther, the headmaster of the Grammar School, acted as curate.

The longest established nonconformist protestant sect in Beverley was Presbyterian. A congregation met from the late 17th century, first in Well Lane and subsequently in Lairgate, where a chapel was built. In the late 18th century the chapel became Independent. The building in use in the mid-Victorian period dated from 1800, and a Sunday school had been added to it in 1821. The manse, now part of County Hall, was almost opposite the chapel. Several prominent families in the town belonged to the Independent Chapel, most notably the Tigars and the Crathornes. In the 1860s the sect extended their activities into the area around the Beck, and used the Temperance Hall, Holme Church Lane, for services.

Methodism flourished in the town in the 19th century: not only were the Wesleyans and the Primitive Methodists well-supported, but there was also a chapel for the United Reform Methodists from 1857, whilst the Church Methodists, the New Connexion Methodists, the Association Methodists, and the Irish Church Methodists all had their adherents in the town at various times. The Wesleyans had two chapels, one in the centre of the town and one near the Beck. In the 19th century the principal chapel, which could hold 700, faced onto Walkergate, with the minister's house and a graveyard in the space between the chapel and Toll Gavel. Several gravestones may still be seen near the present chapel. Many of the industrialists of Beverley were Methodists, including William Crosskill of the ironworks, and Anthony Atkinson, the brickmaker.

Primitive Methodism was very strong in the East Riding, and Beverley had a flourishing congregation, as demonstrated by the building of a new chapel in 1867-8. In the 1850s their original chapel, which had been built in 1825, was in Wednesday Market Place. In the late 1860s the congregation decided that a larger, more imposing building was required. The foundation stone was laid in March 1867, and the chapel was opened in September 1868, with two prayer meetings and a public tea for 1,300 people at the Assembly Rooms. The building was in the Romanesque style, and was constructed of red and white bricks (fig. 27). Internally it was also quite impressive, with a gallery supported by seven maroon pillars, windows with borders of maroon glass, and gas chandeliers. A large schoolroom adjoined the chapel at the back, with four classrooms above it. The chapel itself could accommodate 850, whilst the Sunday school had room for 500 children.

There were two Baptists sects in Beverley in the 19th century. A small Scotch Baptist chapel (now a restaurant) was erected in Swaby's Yard, Walkergate, in 1808. The congregation was only about 50 in 1851, but the sect survived well

26   St. John's Chapel, Lairgate. (East Yorkshire Borough of Beverley Borough Council).

into the 20th century. Particular Baptists began meeting in the late 1820s, and a chapel was erected in 1834 in Well Lane, on a site where Lord Robert's Road now begins. The Society of Friends, or Quakers, had been quite active in the 18th and early 19th centuries. They had a meeting house in Wood Lane, but by the 1830s it had fallen into disuse, and from 1840 was used as a girls' school. Mormons did a little missionary work in the town from their base in Hull.

Beverley's religious tradition was militantly anti-Catholic, as might be expected in a town where nonconformity was so strong and where in addition the Anglican congregations favoured the 'Low Church' rites. In the late 1820s the corporation had been very active in petitioning Parliament against Roman Catholic emancipation. Ironically, in 1850 the town became a Roman Catholic see with its own bishop. The Roman Catholic community in the town was very small at that time. The church, a predecessor of the present one, was situated just outside North Bar. Adjoining it was the priest's house and a small school.

Missionary work played an important role in religious life in the Victorian period. The Church Missionary Society held regular events in Beverley. In December 1859 it organised a 'Christmas Garden' in the Temperance Hall, which was adorned with evergreens, coloured lamps, an 'elegant aquarium', fir trees with stuffed birds sitting on the branches, and cupids in 'shady bowers'. A magic lantern show entertained the visitors, and a sale of work and entrance fees raised £63 0s 3d. Similar events were held annually. Sermons in support of the Society were preached regularly, and visiting missionaries gave accounts of their work. When the Reverend Kirby spoke in St. John's Chapel about his work among the Red Indians, the congregation were moved to tears and it was stated that over the last 38 years £1,216 had been sent from Beverley to the Church Missionary Society.

Other societies with religious connections included the Religious Tract Society and the Society for the Promotion of Christian Knowledge. Both sold religious books and pamphlets in the town. The Sabbath Observance Society and the British Society for the Propagation of the Gospel to the Jews had their adherents. There was a Protestant Association, which sponsored several lectures in the 1850s. Audiences were described as large, and in 1864 an Orange Society Lodge was formed. A tea and festival were held to celebrate the Battle of the Boyne annually for the next few years. In the late 1860s several societies whose programmes were intended to combine religious, social and educational activities were formed in Beverley. The Young Men's Christian Instruction Society was formed under the aegis of the Particular Baptists in 1864. The Young Men's Christian Improvement Society was formed by the Independents in 1866, and the Church Institute was formed by Anglicans in 1867 (see Chapter 7 for further discussion on those societies).

The churches and chapels were closely concerned with the education of the young, and Sunday schools were attached to most places of worship. At a time when the government took little part in education religious bodies played a central role in teaching poorer children the rudiments of reading and writing. To encourage them to attend Sunday schools regularly, social activities, such as outings to the seaside, and games and picnics on Westwood were arranged. In the early 19th century Sunday schools often provided the only education available for the children of the poor, but by mid-century, through the efforts of Anglicans working under the auspices of the National Society for Promoting the Education of the Poor in the Principles of the Established Church (usually shortened to the National Society) and through the efforts of the Wesleyan Methodists, Beverley was well-provided with public elementary schools. There were also numerous private day and boarding schools, varying from high-class establishments providing a classical education for the sons of the upper classes, to small dame schools, some of which merely provided child-minding services.

In Beverley the Grammar School, which might have been expected to provide the best education in the town, was in a moribund state throughout the later 1850s and 1860s, and a new school, the Foundation School, was established in 1861 to cater for the children of the middle classes. There was also a charity school, the Blue Coat School, which catered for poor boys, who went on to be apprentices.

Educational facilities were rather better in Beverley than in many parts of the country: it was recorded in the 1851 census that 1,054 children (657 boys and 397 girls) were on the rolls of the public elementary schools and 471 children (176 boys and 295 girls) were on the rolls of private schools. Nationally 11 per cent of the population were on school rolls, whereas in Beverley the figure was 17 per cent. At that time a child's name on a school roll did not necessarily denote regular attendance, and the census also shows that only about 80 per cent of the children on the rolls were actually in attendance at school in March 1851. Nevertheless the places were provided, and Beverley's record was a creditable one for the period.

The Grammar School was an old foundation, dating back to the Middle Ages. Until the passing of the Municipal Corporations Act of 1835 the school had been aided financially by the corporation, which had paid most of the headmaster's wages. After 1835 the corporation was no longer empowered to carry on that support, and the master was forced to rely upon a small endowment of £10 per annum, from Metcalfe's Charity, and upon money obtained from fees, especially from those for boarding. The fees were raised as a result, and by the 1850s were six guineas for 'free scholars', that is the sons of freemen, and ten guineas plus extras for others. The headmaster lived in an imposing house which is still standing in Keldgate. Until 1816 the school itself was adjacent to the Minster. In that year a new schoolroom of Gothic design (fig. 28) was built next door to the headmaster's house. It consisted of one large room, some 50 feet long and 25 feet wide. The master's desk was at one end and the assistant master's was at the other. There was a porch on the north side with a small library housed in its upper room. The boys also had an extensive playground.

The headmaster from 1845 until 1878 was Charles Easther. At the beginning of his term of office he seems to have been quite successful in attracting boys to the school: the 1851 census shows him to have 11 boarders, and altogether there were 49 scholars. An assistant master was employed at that time. That success was not maintained, and from the mid-1850s there was a sharp decline in the number of scholars. The school's problems were caused by several factors, including the rise in fees, the establishment of the railway, which may have meant some boys going into Hull to school, and the open hostility to the school shown by the Liberals, who were the ruling group on the council until 1867. They considered the school to be elitist, and plans were made to set up a rival establishment. In 1856 Easther was threatened with eviction from his house over a matter which in itself was minor: a dispute over the cataloguing of the school library. Financial problems evidently caused Easther to take on chaplaincy of the workhouse in 1856, and in the 1860s to become the curate of St. Mary's. Those extra duties meant that he had less time to spare for teaching (and by then he had no assistance), and further contributed to the decline of the school. By 1861 there were no boarders, and very few day boys. A report for the Schools Inquiry Commission by Joshua Fitch in 1865 revealed a sorry picture. Fitch reported that the school was 'lifeless and disheartening', the premises were dirty, and the furniture needed repair. There were only 19 scholars, three of them Easther's own sons. The curriculum still included the classics, but the boys were very deficient in all subjects; indeed standards were below those in elementary schools in the town. Somewhat surprisingly a few boys continued to be sent to the school throughout the next decade, but in 1878, when Easther left, it closed, and was not revived until 1890.

The hostility felt by some leading Liberals in mid-century to what they perceived as the exclusivity of the Grammar School led them to explore the possibility of establishing a new 'middle class' school using Susannah Archer's Charity for the relief of 'decayed tradesmen'. The charity was available at that time, since it had just been revealed that the East Riding Registrar had been misappropriating it for some years. A court case to establish the legality of applying the charity to endow a school took almost ten years to progress through the Courts of Chancery, but eventually, in 1860, the new Foundation School was built in Slutwell Lane (now Albert Terrace). The building still stands, being at present used as a health centre, and having been previously used as a fire station.

The school opened in 1861. Pupils were taken from age nine to 13, and could remain until the age of 16. The management was by trustees, who included two clergymen, although the school was non-sectarian. The fees were ten shillings per quarter, and the school was capable of accommodating 80 pupils but was never used to full capacity, there being only about 40 pupils in 1865 rising to about 60 in the 1870s. The syllabus had a practical emphasis, including elementary Latin, suitable for 'children of the lower middle classes', mensuration, geography, and land surveying, together with the usual grammar, arithmetic, reading and writing. In 1865 the pupils' fathers included tanners, builders, and farmers. The headmaster, from the opening of the school until its closure in 1890, was John Ambrose Ridgeway, a certificated teacher from Peterborough. He received £100 per annum, and a rent-free house, which was attached to the school. He also received two thirds of the pupils' fees.

Fitch had commented in 1865 on the excellence of the National schools in Beverley which he said were so good that they vied with the Foundation School for pupils. The town was, from the early 1850s, very well-served by the National Society. Schools established under the auspices of the Church of England were financed by pupils' fees, subscriptions from individuals, fund-raising appeals, sermons, social functions, and, from 1833, by modest government grants. The motives of those supporting such schools were varied. Some were fearful that uneducated people could be unruly. That attitude is well-represented by a comment in 1848 by the Reverend Garret at a meeting to establish St. Mary's Boys' School: 'If we allow the rising population to grow up without being trained in sound and constitutional principles ... in a few years it will be impossible to control them'. That was a common view of middle class people at the time, and was reflected in the central place given to religion in the school

27   Primitive Methodist Chapel, Wednesday Market Place. (Humberside Arts and Leisure).

28   Grammar School, Keldgate. (East Yorkshire Borough of Beverley Borough Council).

curriculum. Some people supported the education of the poorer classes through motives of self-interest, because they needed better-educated workers. Neat copper-plate writing, and arithmetical skills, were required by clerks, shop assistants, and apprentice craftsmen. Other people supported schools because they believed in the value of education for its own sake. Such people favoured the introduction into the curriculum of more interesting subjects, such as geography, history, and music.

There had been two small National schools in the town since the second decade of the century. They were funded principally under the will of James Graves, an incumbent of the Minster, and were closely associated with that church, but children from St. Mary's and St. Nicholas's parishes could also attend. By the 1840s those schools were widely recognised as inadequate. Accordingly there was a flurry of activity in school building in the late 1840s, and a certain amount of rivalry developed between the Minster and St. Mary's. By the mid-1850s there were seven National schools in Beverley.

Three schools were run directly under the auspices of the Minster in the 1850s: Minster Boys' in Lurk Lane; Minster Infants' in Minster Moorgate; and Minster Infants' in Beckside. Minster Boys' School had opened in 1848 in Lurk Lane, just south of the Minster. The building cost £707, and was described as 'neat and substantial', with a capacious classroom, but it was soon found to be too small and was enlarged in 1852 with another classroom being added in 1871. Minster Infants' School in Minster Moorgate was in a building formerly occupied by a charity school established under the will of James Graves. From 1845, though still supported by the Graves's Charity, it became a National school managed by the Minster trustees. The classroom was enlarged in 1871 and rebuilt in 1880. The building still stands and has been converted into a private house. Minster Infants' School, Beckside, was actually in Flemingate, in a new building erected in 1852 and enlarged in 1871. That building too is still standing and is now used as a factory. A fourth school, Graves's Girls' School, was in Minster Yard North. It had been established, under the will of James Graves, in 1810 in Toll Gavel and moved to Minster Yard in 1826. In 1850 the room was enlarged to accommodate 137 pupils, and it was enlarged again in 1863, but was still found to be inadequate, and a nearby room was hired from 1867. From 1861, when the Graves's trustees handed over the management to the Minster, the school became known officially as the Minster National School for Girls. It is now used as the parish rooms.

The clergy and parishioners of St. Mary's were not to be outdone by those of the Minster in the establishment of National schools. An infants' school had been opened in Lairgate in 1838, and was replaced by a new purpose-built school in 1842 (fig. 29). A girls' school in St. Mary's parish had been opened in 1840 in the Quaker meeting house in Wood Lane. It seems to have been associated with St. Mary's, since collections for its upkeep were taken in that church. Boys from St. Mary's parish had been able to attend the Graves's school, but in 1848 a meeting was held of 'influential gentlemen' to consider the establishment of a National school for boys of St. Mary's and St. Nicholas's parishes. As a result subscriptions and donations were made, and a new school, described as a 'useful and ornamental building', and costing £1,026, was erected in 1849 upon the site of the former National school building in Cross Street. That too proved to be too small, and it was enlarged in 1870 and in 1880.

Wesleyan Methodists regarded Sunday schools as an important part of their activities, and by the mid-19th century they were also running day schools. In Beverley they opened a primary school in 1840 in a schoolroom at the back of the chapel in Walkergate and in 1844 a new building was erected in School Lane. The school was for both boys and girls, and entry was not restricted to the children of Methodists. The school was supported by subscriptions, donations and school pence, soon to be augmented by an annual government grant. In 1848 William Spencer came to Beverley as headmaster of the Wesleyan School and remained in that post for 39 years. Under his management the school established a very high reputation. It soon became necessary to extend the building to cope with the demand for places, and that was done in 1859, 1865, and 1872. The original schoolroom was 52 feet long and 26 feet wide. It had a gallery down one side, where children could sit in ranks. Gallery teaching was popular at that time, and was mentioned in several of the elementary school records. It was well-suited to oral teaching and the children took up less space and were easier to control.

The education of Roman Catholic children was catered for in Beverley from 1860 to 1865 in a school attached to St. John's church, North Bar Without. When the marriage of the Prince of Wales and Princess Alexandra of Denmark was celebrated in 1863 the children of the Catholic school were the only ones who did not join in the procession, though 50 commemorative medals were sent along to them. The small population of Catholics in the town and the lack of sufficient funding probably caused the school's closure in 1865.

The staff in most of the public elementary schools consisted of a master or mistress, sometimes one or two assistants if the size of the school merited it, and one or two pupil-teachers. Many of the head teachers stayed for many years: William Spencer has already been mentioned; William Barnard was master of St. Mary's Boys' School from 1855 to 1896; and Thomas Burras was master of the Minster Boys' School from 1868 to 1909. Pupil-teachers were selected from the most promising pupils, and served a five-year apprenticeship. They were expected to attend at about 7 a.m. for lessons from the master or mistress before school began. Despite their lack of experience they usually had charge of a class. Their duties also included making the fire, winding up clocks, getting out books, and stopping in 'with bad or dinner lads'. By the 1850s pupil-teachers who had completed their apprenticeship could proceed on to college, and become certificated teachers. The control of pupil-teachers could cause masters and mistresses considerable trouble. Log books regularly record their lateness or disobedience.

Subjects taught in the elementary schools included the basic skills of reading, writing, and arithmetic, and religious instruction, but by the 1850s history and geography were also being taught. Singing lessons were a regular part of the curriculum, with the emphasis on improving songs, for example 'Little birds and cruel boys' and 'Work hard, help yourselves'. History-teaching in most of the school was probably very dry by modern standards. In the Wesleyan School the methodology used was very similar to that used to teach the catechism — that is by question and answer: Q. Who was Henry VIII? — A. The son of Henry VII. Q. What was his character? A. As a young man he was bluff, generous, right royal, and handsome. Q. How was he when he got older? A. Bloated, vain, cruel, and selfish. If that were typical of a school which had a reputation for high quality teaching, how much more tedious must have been the lessons in the other schools?

After 1862 government grants to public elementary schools were made dependent upon regular attendance and satisfactory peformance in examinations. Subjects tested were reading, writing, arithmetic, and, for girls, needlework. Each child could earn a grant of 4s for attendance, together with 8s for a pass. Children under six were awarded a grant of 6s 6d, based upon a report from the inspector. Capitation grants could tend to restrict the syllabus to only those subjects which were to be examined. The system became known as the Revised Code or Payment by Results. Teachers were also asked to keep log books, which provide useful information upon the conduct of their schools. The new system undoubtedly had a restricting effect upon the curriculum, but some teachers made considerable efforts to include work unrelated to the examinations in their schools.

Provision of the necessary books and writing materials was a constant problem. The younger children wrote upon slates, only progressing to paper when they had reached the higher classes. Text books were constantly in short supply. Some schools augmented the reading material by asking pupils to bring copies of the local newspapers to school. But, as Spencer said when trying to introduce his pupils to current affairs, often there was 'not much taste for reading at home'.

Children were divided into classes by ability rather than age. Class sizes varied but could be quite large: in the Wesleyan School in 1863 there were 55 children in the lowest class (the youngest), and 32 in the first class, but in 1871 when there were over 260 pupils in the school there were 80 children in the fourth class. With such high numbers teachers must have been grateful for less than full attendance.

Attendance at school was not compulsory, and the numbers of those present were subject to wide variation. At the Wesleyan School pupils had to pay whether present or absent, but that was very unusual. Bad weather always kept the numbers low, but the most common causes of absence were the need to work in the fields, and occasional social events. A month's holiday was given at harvest time, varying from year to year according to the weather. But labour was required for other tasks too: in spring weeding, bird-scaring, and other jobs were appropriate for children, and in the summer and autumn hay-making, fruit picking, potato picking, and so on, required extra workers. The timing of the harvest holiday was left to the judgement of the master or mistress. If they miscalculated they could find numbers depleted drastically. Other holidays included about two weeks at Christmas, a week for Easter, and various half holidays, such as Shrove Tuesday, and mayor-choosing day. Unofficial holidays were taken by pupils when other excitements beckoned, such as when a circus was in town or when the Militia held their sports on Westwood. Those affected attendance principally in summertime, whilst in

29   St. Mary's Infants' School, Lairgate. (P. A. Crowther).

30   Former Blue Coat School, Highgate. (P. A. Crowther).

winter snow or rain might keep children away because they lacked appropriate clothing. Infectious diseases were also most prevalent in autumn and winter. In October 1868 only half the children of Beckside Infants were present on account of measles, scarlatina and chicken pox. Typhus and whooping cough were also recorded as reasons for absence. Occasionally the teacher made an entry such as that in the Minster Moorgate Infants' log book for 19 December 1864: 'Lost a little scholar by death'.

School hours usually ran from nine until twelve, and from a quarter to two until half past four. The rules of the Minster Girls' School stated that the door would open at a quarter to nine and close at a quarter past. No-one would be admitted after that. Pupils were to come neat and tidy, with their clothes well-mended or they would be sent home to be made so. Pupils in Victorian schools were generally strictly disciplined, though that was not always easily achieved. Log books record teachers' complaints about noise, problems with truancy, and pupil-teachers' inability to control their classes. Other misdemeanours included arriving at school dirty or not neatly dressed, using bad language, and talking during lessons. Most schools made some use of corporal punishment, but they also used detention, the threat of expulsion, and the memorising of long passages as deterrents. At the Wesleyan School from 1865 a 'Black List' recorded persistent offenders who only had their names removed when they had accumulated several good marks. In 1867 William Spencer decided to have an experimental month without using corporal punishment and when the month was up he abolished it for the top two classes unless they were on the Black List. St. Mary's Infants' School was organised under Samuel Wilderspin's system, which emphasised character training and good manners, but avoided corporal punishment.

The usual age for starting infants' school was five, but some children were sent earlier, particularly if there were older brothers or sisters to take them. The inspector's report for Beckside Infants' School in 1864 stated that it 'would be well if not so many very young infants were admitted'. The transfer from the infants' to the boys' or girls' school took place at about seven. The age of leaving varied according to family circumstances. In January 1858 a list of boys leaving the Minster School included six, aged between 11 and 14, who left school to go to work, six who left the town, six who left because of irregular attendance, and one eight year old who left 'through distress'. Girls tended to leave school earlier than boys: the 1851 census reported that 'girls are taken away from schools at an early age for household duties'. At the Wesleyan School Spencer recorded that 'many girls are entered but a great number stay too short a time to do any good'.

The fees were an important consideration for parents. Education at that time was not free, and at all the public elementary schools pupils had to pay a penny, or more usually two pence, weekly. The large numbers of Beverley children in the elementary schools perhaps testifies to the truth of one inspector's report on the town that 'there is a large number of well-paid operatives, temperate enough to be able to pay for their children's education, intelligent enough to value it'. At the Minster Boys' School in 1859 the subsiding of scholars was being considered. Any boy nominated by a member of the school committee was to pay half fees, with his nominator paying the rest. An alternative suggestion was that the pupil's parents should pay the full fees, but have part returned if attendance had been regular. The latter system seems to have been adopted. At many schools the first child to enter the school paid the full fee, with subsequent children being given lower rates.

Several charity schools had been opened in the town in the 18th and early 19th centuries. Those opened under the will of James Graves have already been mentioned. The Blue Coat School, which was intended for poor children, particularly those orphaned, had been established in the early 18th century. Girls and boys attended the school in the 18th century, but by the 19th century only boys were eligible. The numbers of scholars fluctuated: in the early 18th century there were about 30, but throughout the 19th century there were between six and ten boys in the school. However in the mid-Victorian period there were usually several day boys, whose fees augmented the master's income. The school was situated in Highgate, in buildings which still stand (fig. 30).

There were several private schools in Beverley. The most long-lasting was that of Miss Elizabeth Stephenson, which she had established in Eastgate with her sister Ellen, in the 1820s. In 1851 the school occupied a house in Hengate. The census records that there were 34 boarders, four of whom were the nieces of the Miss Stephensons. All the boarders except four were girls, with ages ranging from six to 18. Their places of birth ranged from Hull, and all three ridings of Yorkshire, to as far afield as Scotland. Two Legard brothers, Algernon Willoughby and Cecil Henry aged eight and seven, who were scholars here, were probably being prepared for public school. The school already had a high reputation, which it maintained until the end of its existence. It was later, c.1866, to move to Holland House, Register Square, where it remained until it closed in 1926.

The majority of the private schools in the town in mid-century catered for young ladies, and offered subjects regarded as suitable for their status in society. Ladylike accomplishments such as French, music, drawing, dancing and calisthenics frequently featured in advertisements. Miss Whitwham of Railway Street, stated that 'every effort will be made to impart to the young ladies an accomplished and Christian education'. The boys' private schools tended to be aimed at a slightly lower class, since upper class boys would probably have been sent to better public schools than Beverley had to offer. Advertisements for boys' schools emphasised commercial and mercantile skills. In 1857 Mr. George Dook of Wednesday Market Place advertised the opening of his Commercial School, where boys would be taught English, grammar, writing, arithmetic, geography, book-keeping, mensuration and land surveying, for ten to fifteen shillings per quarter if day pupils, and five to six pounds if boarders. At Ivy House boarding and day school, which was situated on the corner of Minster Moorgate and Lairgate, pupils could live with the family, and partake of a diet 'excellent and unlimited', for 18 guineas per annum if under ten, and 20 guineas if above it. Subjects taught included:

English in all its branches, and especially dictation to improve spelling, geography, practical land surveying, arithmetic, mercantile correspondence, book-keeping by single and double entry, themes in the form of letters, drawing, dancing, and drilling ...

Beverley had a wide range of schools catering for the children of all classes. Their parents had often not been so fortunate, and there were many adults in the town who felt that their education needed augmenting. In 1863 the master and assistant master of the Minster Boys' School started an evening school for adults on three evenings a week from seven until nine. The subjects taught were reading, writing, arithmetic, and if required, book-keeping, mensuration, algebra and drawing. Fees were 4d per week or 1½d per night. In March 1864 the evening school closed for a time because the numbers (13) were deemed to be too low. However it started up again, and in 1866 the inspector reported that it was flourishing, but that:

I would recommend a little more correct discipline to be exercised. The time occupied in work is not long, therefore the continual talking while engaged at work should be firmly discouraged.

Maintaining discipline with adults must have been a difficult matter. In 1869 the inspector stated that the night scholars passed their test '... fairly well, [but] reading and spelling need a good deal of care and attention'. In addition to that class, as will be seen in the next chapter, several organisations sprang up to meet the demand for adult education: among them were the Mechanics' Institute, the Mutual Improvement Society, the Church Institute, and the Young Men's Christian Improvement and Instruction Societies.

CHAPTER SEVEN
SOCIAL LIFE AND 'IMPROVEMENT'

The types of social activity to be found in Beverley catered for all classes and ranged from eminently refined and respectable gatherings to the simpler pleasures of the tap-room. The Assembly Rooms provided accommodation for events demanding extensive space, such as flower shows, theatrical entertainments, panoramas, dances, and concerts, and for more intimate functions such as chess clubs, card parties and lectures. Beverley had no permanent theatre in mid-century, but travelling companies rented the Assembly Rooms or the Mechanics' Institute Hall, or sometimes brought their own temporary wooden buildings to set up in a field, often at the back of an inn. The search after improvement via education spawned a multiplicity of societies and associations, most notably the Mechanics' Institute and the Mutual Improvement Society. The numerous inns, public houses, and beer houses offered conviviality, drink, and sometimes entertainment, and were the meeting places for friendly societies and clubs. The Victorian concern about drunkenness and its accompanying evils was reflected in a very flourishing temperance movement, which offered, to those who were prepared to give up alcohol, alternative evening activities, such as revival-type meetings, tea parties, concerts, and improving talks.

The Assembly Rooms had been built in Norwood in the 1760s, to serve the requirements of a more elegant age. Balls, assemblies, and card parties were held there for their middle and upper class patrons. The main assembly room itself was 50 feet by 27, whilst the tea room and the card room were much smaller. By the Victorian period public rooms on a much larger scale were required, particularly for the accommodation of the shows held by the Beverley and East Riding Agricultural Society and the Floral and Horticultural Society. In 1839 a committee was appointed to oversee the building of a new hall, to be erected in a garden at the back of the old Rooms. As in the 18th century the building was to be financed by shares, and a limit of £2,500 was set for the cost. The architect was H. F. Lockwood, who produced a lithograph of the interior (fig. 31). Apparently modelled on Roman baths, it consisted of one lofty room 88 feet long, 53 feet wide and 41 feet high, with five bays, each topped by a semi-circular window, and ornate interior decorations. It is the shell of that building which remains today. When the old Assembly Rooms were pulled down in 1935 the 'new' Rooms were divided into two storeys, the upper one becoming a ball-room, and the lower one being converted to a cinema (the Regal).

The new building, formally known as the Beverley and East Riding Public Rooms, was opened in July 1840, with an agricultural show followed by a dinner for 800 persons, which was supplied by the landlord of the King's Arms. The Rooms were lit by gas, heated by coal and coke, and ovens and hot plates were installed. Ample seating was provided for the concerts, lectures, and theatrical entertainments which took place there. The large room was ideally suited for the accommodation of formal balls, and many organisations used it for that purpose. The Holderness Hunt held its annual ball in the Rooms, as did the Freemasons, and there were Race, Trade, Archery Club, and friendly society balls. Dancing was a favourite Victorian recreation, and the dancing masters who held classes in the Rooms found a ready market. In the 1850s regular quadrille parties were held in the Rooms, to introduce the 'newest and most fashionable dances [under] the strictest order'. In 1866 the members of the 'Original Royal Tribe of Gypsies' gave notice in the newspapers that they were going to hold a Gypsey Ball on 18th December. A first class quadrille band was engaged, and the gypsies appeared in costume, accompanied by their King and Queen.

Dinners for large numbers were held regularly in the Rooms. Catering was undertaken by local innkeepers, most frequently by Francis Burrell of the nearby White Horse. When a dinner for a Beverley M.P. was planned applications were requested early so that Mr. Burrell could make suitable preparation for the meal, which had as its main course game supplied from local landowners' estates. Over 350 sat down to dinner. The large room was decorated for the Masonic Ball in 1858 with:

> *evergreens, flowers, statuary, vases, Masonic pedestals and emblematic devices ... A light and tastefully ornamented verandah round the room served as a promenade. The colours of the East Riding Militia, and those of the Beverley Volunteer Corps were placed in conspicuous positions – the whole producing a more pleasing and classic effect than have ever been alllowed in that large room before.*

The East Yorkshire Militia, which was mustered every May for manoeuvres on Westwood, held its dinner and ball in the Rooms, and the accounts show that after that event breakages were regularly paid for by the officers, suggesting a certain amount of disorder. The Rifle Volunteers also used the Rooms for meetings and indoor drills.

Many Beverley clubs and societies made use of the Rooms. Friendly societies such as the Oddfellows and the Foresters held meetings and social events there. A multiplicity of religious societies flourished in the town in mid-Victorian times. Such societies using the Rooms for meetings included the Church Missionary Society, the Society for the Propagation of the Gospel, the Protestant Association and many others. Recreational and educational clubs using the Rooms included the Chess Club, the Mutual Improvement Society, the Church Institute, the Archery Club, the Choral Society, the Hibernian Society, and the Irish Society. An annual event held in the Rooms and the adjoining gardens of Norwood House was the exhibition of the Beverley and East Riding Poultry Association which had been formed in early 1858. After 1862 the Association broadened its range of interests, and changed its name to the Beverley and East Riding Poultry, Floral and Horticultural Society. The show by that time had become a popular social event.

Beverley's last theatre, which was in Lairgate, closed in 1840 but travelling theatrical companies continued to visit the town and usually hired the large room. Performances ranged from farces to Shakespearean drama, very often on the same bill, as on the night of July 25th 1854, when the Shakespearean tragedy of Richard III was followed by a song by Miss Agnes MacDonald, and 'The screaming farce of the haunted heath'. There were three types of seats, the front were two shillings, the pit was one shilling, and the back seats were sixpence. Those people who wished to avoid the more serious dramas, which tended to precede the interval, could arrive at nine o'clock and be admitted for half price in time for the farce. Speciality acts, such as ventriloquists, illusionists, magicians, and a practitioner of the Indian rope trick, were seen regularly.

Panoramas were a popular form of Victorian entertainment, and several visited Beverley in the 1850s and 1860s. In a panorama a cylinder, of about 60 feet or more, is covered with an accurate painting of a landscape, so that an observer standing or sitting in the centre of the cylinder sees the picture like an actual landscape in nature completely surrounding him in all directions. This gives an effect of great reality to the picture, which is often skilfully aided in various ways. The observer may be on a platform representing, say, the flat roof of a house, and the space between the platform and the picture is covered with real objects which gradually blend into the picture itself. The picture is lighted from above, but a roof is spread over the central platform so that no light but that reflected from the picture reaches the eye. To make the light appear the more brilliant, the passages and staircase which lead the spectator to the viewing place are often kept nearly dark.

The panoramas which came to the Rooms included 'The Arctic Regions', 'Australian Views', and 'African Views'. In June 1857 it was announced that M. Gompertz, the proprietor and artist of the Panorama of the Arctic Regions, and of the Crypt of the Holy Sepulchre of Jerusalem, would exhibit his panorama of the late war (the Crimean). The exhibition was preceded by a pictorial chart of the Crimea, so that the spectators could orientate themselves to the various scenes depicted. That was followed by a series of views, including Constantinople, the Bosphorus with the combined fleets at anchor, the Black Sea by moonlight, the 'barbarous massacre at Sinope', the cavalry charge at Balaklava, and so on. A sax-horn band and singers together with a descriptive lecture completed the entertainment.

Public lectures took place in the Rooms regularly. One, on the electric telegraph, held in February 1858, excited particular interest. In order to demonstrate the new means of communication, an electric cable was carried across the town from the railway station 'much to the astonishment of the humbler classes, and a great number of juveniles'. During the lecture telegraphic messages were received from York and London, the latter including a few words of a speech which was then being delivered in the House of Commons. Musical entertainments, whether provided by Beverlonians themselves, or by travelling companies, were regular events. Mr. Frederick Bartle, the proprietor of a music shop in Beverley, was a frequent performer and organiser of amateur concerts. Professionals included Dr. Mark and his Little Men, a company of boys between the ages of five and ten years, consisting of 30 instrumentalists and a chorus of 40. They were described as 'extremely clever youngsters ... two or three not more than two feet in height ... the star being Master Sturge whose solos on the cornet were enchanting'. The Ethiopian Singers and the Christie Minstrels also visited Beverley.

The Mechanics' Institute movement began in the 1820s as an attempt to compensate for the working classes' lack of education, especially of a technical or scientific nature. The movement spread rapidly, and by 1840 there were 300 institutes throughout the country, many of themn with purpose-built halls for lectures and classes, libraries, and newspaper rooms. The Beverley Mechanics' Institute began in 1832, with the Mayor chairing a meeting in the Minster parish rooms, which was attended by 150 'operatives'. At a further meeting that year support from the 'more opulent and leading members of the community' was requested. The comment was made that there was a rising population of operatives and apprentices in the town, who ought to have their 'vacant hours employed in a profitable and improving manner, not wasted in idle and frivolous amusement or worse, wasted in debauchery'. A total of 85 members was enrolled: honorary members paid 3 guineas and 10s 6d p.a., ordinary members paid 1s in advance and 4s 6d in instalments.

In the early years the Minster parish rooms continued to be used for meetings, but it was soon agreed that a hall was required to accommodate the various activities planned. In 1837 Beverley Corporation was paid £50 for ground in Register Square, and the Hall, built in an imposing classical style at a cost of about £1,500 (raised in £1 shares), was opened in 1842 (fig. 32). Additions to it, comprising a library, reading room, raised platform, and seating, were made in 1844. In 1850 it was said that classrooms were needed to provide for more practical classes, but those were never built. The Hall does not seem to have ever been finished as planned. The library, which was originally to include 'no plays, novels, romances, divinity, or politics', proved very popular. Works of popular literature were later allowed, and by 1852 the library contained over one thousand books, with five thousand issued during the year. The reading room opened four nights per week, and subscriptions were taken out for three weekly and nine monthly periodicals. However one member described the reading room in 1857 as 'cheerless and uncomfortable' and said that the papers were not kept up to date and no local or national newspapers were taken. The Institute had a museum, begun in 1833. Various objects were added from time to time, including the head of an Egyptian mummy which was presented in 1858.

The lectures held in the Institute were given by 'resident gentlemen of scientific and literary attainments' as well as by visitors. Local speakers included medical practitioners, such as Dr. Sandwith, who spoke on such diverse topics as 'Insects injurious to health', 'Moral training', and 'The economy of nature', and Dr. Brereton, whose speciality seems to have been geology, and whose topics included 'Mineralogy', and 'A cobble stone'. Joseph Hind, a prominent Liberal, spoke on political or educational matters, and a solicitor and councillor, H. Sylvester, gave lectures on education and literature. A 'working mechanic' from Beverley, J. F. Wynn, gave several talks, including one on 'Love and marriage, or woman's mission'. Scientific and technical lectures seem to have been the most popular: between 1850 and the late 1860s such lectures comprised one third of the programme, with literature a poor second. However in 1852 it was stated that many of the lectures were 'too scientific to be understood by those unversed in the sciences'. Perhaps to enliven their talks several speakers used illustrative material: C. Beckett of Hull Medical School was accompanied by a real skeleton for 'A conversation with a skeleton'; Dr. Child of Leeds Mechanics' Institute entertained the audience with experiments in electricity and galvanism.

Literary topics included Shakespeare, Dickens, Oliver Goldsmith, Daniel Defoe, *Uncle Tom's Cabin* (then recently published), and 'Frolicsome caprices of fun and fancy' in which the lecturer rambled 'at liberty over the extensive field of modern literature' moving the audience 'to roars of laughter, quiet smiles, intense feeling'. Current affairs and politics were regular topics: they included 'A general view of Great Britain's colonial empire', and 'Our country, and its advantages, or the superiority of Great Britain over other nations', a lecture by Joseph Hind which must have given great satisfaction to its hearers. A lecture in November 1851 drew a full audience, the subject being 'The present state of female costume, illustrating the changes of fashion during the last three centuries'. The speaker, Julia Lester, was an advocate of Bloomerism, a fashion introduced by Amelia Bloomer in 1849, involving the wearing of a short skirt with loose trousers, gathered around the ankles. A lady in full Bloomer dress of black velvet was present to illustrate the talk.

The lectures tended to attract a rather middle-class audience, described in newspaper reports as 'fashionable', 'respectable', or 'of the superior caste'. But the Institute had been formed to attract working people, and classes of a more basic educational nature were run from time to time. In the late 1840s there was instruction in drawing, music, practical mechanics and arithmetic, which attracted 87 students. In the early 1850s there were discussion and essay groups. It was said that many members who now spoke frequently and fluently in public attributed their success to those classes. The composition and essay classes apparently attracted 'a fair proportion of tradesmen and mechanics', but it was said that more practical courses were needed to help such people in their trades. Annual soirées for class members were held in the library and reading room, with tea, speeches, songs and recitations. In 1856 a band was formed, but apparently appeared in public somewhat prematurely, since the *Beverley Guardian* stated that 'the band, in its present crude state, is anything but a source of pleasure to the audience' and suggested that more labour 'in private might perhaps render it endurable, ... at present its performances are most excruciating'. Progress seems to have been rapid however: only a few weeks later the band was praised by the same newspaper for overcoming difficulties, and having only a few 'trifling defects'. Thereafter the band played at many events in the town. In 1857 it gave monthly concerts in the Hall, with the Beverley Harmonic Society.

The highest figure for members of the Institute was 360, recorded in 1847, but thereafter membership gradually declined. In 1852 subscriptions totalled only half of the amount raised in 1849, not even enough to cover expenditure. By that period many societies were being formed in Beverley, and they were

31 New Public Rooms (interior). Lithograph by H. F. Lockwood. (East Yorkshire Borough of Beverley Borough Council).

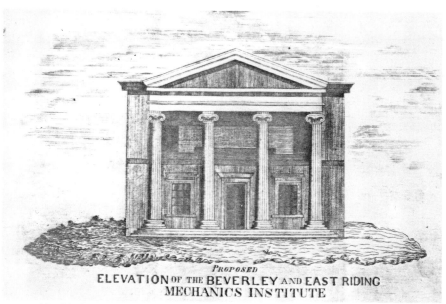

PROPOSED
ELEVATION OF THE BEVERLEY AND EAST RIDING
MECHANICS INSTITUTE

32 Mechanics' Institute, Cross Street. (Humberside County Archives Office).

perhaps attracting members away. In 1852 over £20 was raised by letting the Hall for other purposes. It was stated at the annual meeting that the Institute had been in a 'low and almost deserted position' for three to four years. At a discussion calling for ideas to strengthen membership the lectures were criticised for being too scientific or dry, and wearying the audiences. Other attractions were needed or 'the lethargic people of Beverley will let the Institute fall into such obscurity that nothing but the brick walls of the fabric will remain as a memento that such an Institute ever existed in this town'. It was decided to arrange more classes, reorganise the library, and arrange an improved lecture session in the hope of achieving better attendances. An exhibition was also held in 1852 to stimulate interest in the Institute. Works of art, curiosities, and models of Crosskill's carts, waggons and agricultural implements as shown at the Great Exhibition, were assembled for display.

In 1855 the annual meeting was a difficult one; it was alleged that some members were trying to break up the Institute, and there were charges of mismanagement. At a second, more harmonious meeting, subscriptions were raised to try to pay off debts. In 1857 membership fees were 1s 6d per quarter, but for ladies and young persons 1s a quarter. The financial position had improved by 1858, when it was announced that income exceeded expenditure, and that there were 222 members. It was recorded that the experiment of having monthly soirées had, on the whole, been successful, and the lectures were described as being varied and interesting. Nevertheless by the early 1860s the Hall was only being used irregularly, and then most often by other societies. It seems that other societies were usurping the Institute's role and that the founders had lost their initial enthusiasm. By 1870 the Mechanics' Institute's building had fallen into disuse and it was eventually demolished in 1890 and the new County Hall was erected on the site.

In the mid-19th century a society flourished in the town whose name is redolent of the Victorian preoccupation with self-improvement. The Mutual Improvement Society was formed in November 1852 by seven young men, who resolved to meet regularly in each other's houses for discussion, essay-reading, and lectures. They may have modelled themselves upon such societies formed in the West Riding in the 1840s. The Society was conducted, with varying success, in a private manner until 1856, when it was decided to make it public in order to extend its usefulness. The meeting place from November of that year became the Temperance Hotel in Wednesday Market. The fourth anniversary was celebrated with a soirée on 5th December, for members and friends. Satisfactory progress was made during 1857, with nine discussions, seven essay-readings, and three lectures.

On the 26th November 1857 the Society, keeping its own name, amalgamated with the short-lived Mutual Instruction Society, and in December the first public soirée was held to celebrate the fifth anniversary. Nearly 200 people were present, ladies being in the majority and 'among whom were noticed stately dames and beauteous damsels, many of the latter appearing in concert in costume'. Mr.Grainger, one of the oldest members, said that the present age had made much progress in arts and sciences, and that young men ought to embrace opportunities to improve their minds and better their condition. They would not be at a loss to know how to spend a leisure hour. There would be plenty of subjects for consideration, and membership would fit them for higher offices in society, perhaps qualify them to become members of the Corporation.

The soirées were held in the Public Rooms and attracted large numbers of people. The proceedings began with tea, taken in the small room, which was decorated with banners and mottoes, but was said to be rather too small to accommodate 250 comfortably. After the meal the company moved to the large room for dancing, whilst the small room was prepared for a concert. Speeches, songs, madrigals, and orations followed, and then all moved back to the large room for more dancing. However the serious business of the Society took place during the weekly meetings. Occasionally the voting after discussions was recorded in the newspapers, and that together with the titles of the discussions, makes instructive reading. The subjects ranged from politics, through history, to family life and morals. Political questions included whether Jews should be admitted to Parliament (no), whether England would be better without railways (yes), and whether Beverley should lose one of its M.P.s (no, narrowly). Members were asked to consider whether the introduction of machinery had benefited the working classes (yes), whether turnpikes ought to be abolished (no), and which most deserves the esteem of mankind, the poet, the statesman, or the warrior (the statesman). Moral questions included whether horse-racing was injurious to the morality of the country (no), whether riches or poverty were more productive of crime (riches), and whether any circumstances can justify a departure from the truth (no). The subjects set for essays were equally varied: Mirth, Independence, Early closing, Mutual Improvement Societies, Christmas, Gambling, War, Manhood, and Happiness.

The question of the admission of women came up several times. In 1859 the chairman had expressed the hope that a ladies' society would be established, and the secretary, who had obviously made some comments on that issue on an earlier occasion, said he was sorry if he had given any offence, or had been the means of keeping any of the fair sex away, but he held the same opinion as he had then, which was:

> *that the proper sphere for ladies was at home, where they might be instructed in the art of cooking. The only way of getting at an Englishman's affections was through his stomach, and no other place, and if that is suitably provided for, matters will go on pleasantly. The other day he had been out rather late, and when he returned home his tea was not ready, whereby he lost his temper ... Women might be of assistance in persuading their husbands and brothers to join the Society (ladies had great influence on the mind of man).*

The chairman responded by saying that he should not want ladies to be always in the kitchen, and must say that if he had a wife he should treat her as a companion and not as a slave. Most members, however, seemed to think that the rightful role for the ladies was to appear at the soirées 'looking even more tempting than the delicacies before them', and attend to the wants of the inner man. They were also required to persuade their menfolk to join the Society, which would turn them into 'good husbands and thinking and moral men' who would do well in the world.

The fortunes of the Mutual Improvement Society fluctuated throughout its life span. By the early 1860s appeals were being made for new members, and the Society seems to have been failing. In February 1868 at a special meeting it was unanimously resolved that the Society should be dissolved. Members concluded that to try and keep up their ranks was impracticable in view of the 'apathy of the young men of the town'. It was stated that such a step had been taken only after 'protracted consideration, and not without reluctance'. The reason given was the establishment of literary societies in connection with religious bodies.

Those societies included the Young Men's Christian Instruction Society, which began in January 1864, in association with the Baptist Chapel. The lectures were of a predominantly religious nature, but also included some literary topics. Politics were occasionally discussed, notably in March 1867, when the discussion was entitled 'Trade unions — are they beneficial?'. Several working men took part and a large majority of the meeting voted in favour of the unions. Penny readings were a regular part of the programme, as were poems and songs, which were accompanied by a harmonium. In early 1866, when the Mutual Improvement Society was struggling to survive, the meetings of the Young Men's Christian Instruction Society were so well-attended that some people were unable to obtain admission. In October of that year plans were made by the Society to open a working mens' club with rooms for conversation, writing, chess and draughts, and for newspapers, magazines, and books. In November such a club opened in a house in Sow Hill, with hours from 6.30 to 10 p.m. on Wednesdays, and from 1 p.m. on Saturdays. In February 1868 the Society held a soirée at the Public Rooms, at which it was stated that since the inauguration there had been 23 public lectures and 110 meetings, principally discussions, conversations, essays, readings, and recitations. The same period had also see the inauguration of a singing club, a cricket club and a library of about 250 volumes.

In October 1866 the Young People's Christian Improvement Society, established in connection with the Independent Chapel, Lairgate, was founded. By January 1867 it had changed its name to the Young Men's Christian Improvement Society, though whether that was to specifically exclude women, or because it had failed to attract them, is not known. It too had a programme which included lectures, penny readings, and concerts. It used the schoolrooms of the Independent Chapel, the Baptist Chapel, and the Mechanics' Institute and the Public Rooms for its meetings.

An Anglican rival to those societies began in early 1867, with the establishment of the Church Institute. When the Mechanics' Institute collapsed, and nonconformist educational societies began to fill the gap, Beverley Anglicans apparently felt that it was time to establish their own society. An inaugural soirée was held at the Assembly Rooms, presided over by the mayor, and attended by 'representatives of divinity, medicine, and the law'.

The mayor, H. E. Sylvester, said that the objects of the Institute were:

the improvement of its members in all branches of science, including theology and ecclesiastical government as taught by the Church of England, and a cultivation of a taste for literature and the fine arts.

The promoters said that mechanics' institutes had attracted tradesmen, clerks, and the middle classes, rather than the mechanics for whom they had been founded. They intended to offer such attractions as would keep the young from the public house and off the streets, as well as give them educational opportunities. A library, a reading room and newsroom, chess groups, and meetings for 'mutual improvement' would be offered to members.

A house in Toll Gavel was rented but by November it was found to be too small, and arrangements were made to take the adjacent house in addition. In January 1868 the Institute moved into Ann Routh's house, no. 45 Toll Gavel, and the house adjoining. There was not a sufficiently large room in either house for 'entertainments', so the Assembly Rooms continued to be used for lectures and readings. Those events were extremely well-attended: in February 1868 a reading and concert was attended by between 500 and 600 people.

Throughout the late 1860s the Institute flourished: in January 1869 there were 200 members. Its rooms were well-furnished, warmed, and lighted, and provided with newspapers, periodicals, and books. There was a special room set apart for ladies, 'guarded' from the menfolk by Mrs. Wilson who looked after the house. There was even a smoking room set aside for members who would feel uncomfortable 'if deprived of their favourite weed'. This, said the chairman, had anticipated railway legislation. The house was open from 9 a.m. to 10 p.m. Classes in reading, drawing, and discussion groups were run by seniors for the younger members.

The Church Institute had a varied programme, which covered history, science, and politics, with religious matters playing quite a minor part. There were excursions to Fountains Abbey, Chatsworth, Harrogate and Ripon. In January 1870 a grand amateur gymnastic entertainment and assault-at-arms was staged. There was a capacity audience in the Assembly Rooms to see feats of swordsmanship, wrestling, trapeze, and other acrobatic acts.

In February 1859 the Beverley Natural History Society was formed. At the first meeting a paper on butterflies and moths was read by the Secretary. In October the Society's committee called for support from the local nobility and gentry. Cases and cabinets for displaying specimens in a future museum were being assembled, and the Society requested subscriptions, donations, books, and specimens of any branch of natural history. The annual subscription rates were six shillings for ordinary members (including ladies), four shillings for youths and apprentices, and one guinea for honorary members. At the end of the first year donations to the museum included a collection of fossil plants and 'plastic clay formations', seven species of birds, and a collection of war spears, hunting spears and knives from Borneo. In April 1859 a mahogany cabinet with a collection of 1,110 British beetles, 200 specimens of exotic beetles, and 250 shells from Scarborough and district, was presented. A large buzzard, shot at Gransmoor, was also added to the collection. In December 1860 a meeting was held at which prizes were given for the best collection of insects. There was to have been a prize for the best essay on a natural history subject, but none was submitted. Indeed there seems to have been a very luke-warm response to the Natural History Society. In February 1861 it was said that there had been a very limited response from 'our influential neighbours', and want of funds was holding back development. Interest had been shown by young people, particularly of the working classes, who had read and re-read the small library, but because of the shortage of books their interest had died, and the lack of cabinets for exhibits, and money to fund public lectures meant that the Society might have to be terminated. That may have been its fate, since it is not mentioned thereafter in the press.

Several libraries were established in association with the societies of the period. There were also circulating libraries in the town, run by booksellers, notably Green's in Saturday Market Place (which survived well into this century), and Ward's in Wednesday Market Place. In addition the Subscription, News, and Billiards Rooms, which had been built in Cross Street in 1830, were still flourishing in mid-Victorian times, as was a Conservative newsroom in North Bar Within.

Beverley's numerous inns, taverns, and beerhouses played a central role in the town's social life. They varied considerably in status. At the top end of the scale were the larger inns, providing accommodation as well as refreshments, and catering for the middle and upper classes. The taverns and alehouses, which formed the largest group, were diverse in size and clientèle. Some were quite large, with additional rooms which were let out for dinners to groups like friendly societies, others were very small, often with only one public room, though in such taverns the customers might also drink in the landlord's private quarters. The humblest establishments were the beerhouses, which were operated under the Beerhouses Act of 1830, whereby any householder paying poor rates was allowed to sell beer without a magistrates' licence. Such a system allowed persons in lowly circumstances to make a living by selling their own home-brewed beer in their front parlour.

Between 1850 and the late 1860s the number of inns and taverns fluctuated very little: in 1851 the directory listed 36, whilst in 1867 there were 37. The borough magistrates, who held brewsters' sessions every September, kept a careful watch over licensed premises. They cautioned, or withdrew licences from landlords who let their premises be used for gambling, or kept an unruly house. By contrast with the inns and taverns there was a marked increase in the number of beerhouses over the same period: in 1851 there were eight, whereas in 1867 there were 25. If all the establishments offering alcohol are added together it appears that in 1851 there was one for every 212 persons, and in 1871 one for every 165 persons.

The inns and taverns (fig. 3) were clustered quite thickly in the centre of the town, with five in Saturday Market Place, four in Ladygate, three in Toll Gavel, Lairgate, and North Bar Within, and either one or two in Butcher Row, Hengate, Norwood, and North Bar Without. In Ladygate three of the four taverns, the Freemason's Arms, the Lion and Lamb, and the Globe, were more or less next door to each other. There was a similar concentration in the industrial area of the town, towards the Beck, with three in Flemingate, and five in Beckside. Those in or near Saturday Market Place were used by carriers on Saturdays to drop and pick up passengers and goods. The Globe's landlord owned a pig market at the back of his property, and many taverns were used for the sale of horses and other livestock. The Beckside taverns were much used by boatmen and tannery workers.

The Beverley Arms, the King's Head, the King's Arms (fig. 33), the Pack Horse, the Cross Keys, and the Holderness Hotel (now Schofield's), were the principal inns of the period, and catered for the upper and middle classes. Respectable women could enter those establishments without fear of censure. In the second rank were the smaller inns, which catered mainly for the agricultural and commercial classes. The Globe, the White Horse, the Green Dragon, the Rose and Crown, and the Valiant Soldier amongst others, were quite large houses which could provide accommodation and meals as well as alcoholic drinks. Some inns were well placed for business of a specialised kind: when the Rose and Crown was put on sale in 1853 it was advertised as being set at the junction of the York and Driffield roads, and 'in immediate connection with all places of public business, particularly when fairs, races and sessions are held'. That inn, with its extensive stabling, was also used for the accommodation of race horses and hunters, and many sales of horses and ponies took place in its yards. Pleasure was easily combined with business in such places.

Beerhouses were supposed to close at ten in the evenings, but there were no restrictions on the hours of opening of inns and taverns, except during 'the hours of divine service' on Sundays. In 1858 it was reported that a man and woman stayed drinking in the Plough, Flemingate, until 4 a.m. Such late hours were exceptional, and most taverns probably closed at about eleven. Several of the public houses in Ladygate were rather rough and rowdy establishments, and their customers did not always disperse at closing time, but congregated on corners causing a disturbance and sometimes associating with prostitutes. The police did not usually concern themselves with minor infringements of the peace, but had to step in when complaints about bad behaviour became too frequent.

Beerhouses were predominantly drinking places, and some were very temporary establishments. Many, however, thrived, put up signs with their names, and remained in operation for several years. The Spotted Cow beerhouse was in Wednesday Market Place, and other establishments with evocative names such as the Frog and Frying Pan, the Tally Ho, the Three Merry Women, and the New Found Out were remembered by George Armstrong, a Beverley butcher writing at the end of the 19th century.

Many landlords brewed their own beer but for those who wished to buy in their beer there were several breweries in the town. In 1851 they included the Golden Ball Brewery situated at the rear of the Golden Ball public house in Toll Gavel and owned by Robert Stephenson and Son, the East Riding Brewery in Butcher Row owned by George Stephenson, and the Ladygate Brewery owned by Henry Johnson. Those who wanted a change from the local

33   King's Arms, North Bar Within. (Stuart Witty).

34   Former Temperance Hall, Champney Road. (P. A. Crowther).

brews could obtain Guinness at the Holderness Hotel, and 'London stout' and 'Burton pale ale' from Robinson's shop (Push) in the Market Place.

As at the present day, some landlords were tenants whilst others owned their premises. The changeover of tenancy was very rapid for some establishments: between 1851 and 1858 two thirds (24 of the 36) inns and taverns changed hands. By contrast there were one or two establishments which stayed in the same hands or with the same families for decades. The Angel, Butcher Row, was managed by Daniel Boyes from the 1840s until the 1870s, and the White Horse, Hengate, was tenanted by the Burrell family more or less throughout the 19th century, whilst the Morley family held the Beverley Arms from 1852 until 1920.

Throughout the 19th century the foremost inn in the town was the Beverley Arms, whose high social status was undisputed. It was in a good position opposite St. Mary's church, had ample stabling and outbuildings, its own brewery, and large gardens and a paddock where circuses occasionally put up their tents. The extensive kitchens (later to be immortalised by Beverley painter Frederick Elwell) were required to cater for the formal dinners which took place at the inn quite frequently. The annual banquet of the Holderness Hunt, Beverley Race Committee dinners, and the entertainment of Humbert, Crown Prince of Italy, must have demanded much of the landlord and staff. The elevated tone sought by the Beverley Arms was appreciated by a visitor in the 1860s. Edwin Waugh, the travel writer, stayed at the inn for a few days and remarked upon its 'cleanliness, bounty, and genial comfort'. Its position impressed him, 'in the town, but in a serene and pleasant nook'. The proximity of St. Mary's according to Waugh:

> seemed to affect the language and dignity of the customers ... and of the servants who attended them. The waiters whispered, with a reverential air, as if it was close upon service time ... The Beverley Arms might have been the vestry of a church ... there was a cloistral calm about the whole place. It was like sitting in some old monastic refectory; and the landlord himself had something of the quaintness and subdued geniality of an ancient cellarer.

Waugh might have taken a different impression away with him had he arrived during election time, when the Beverley Arms, a Conservative inn, was a hive of activity. Candidates were accommodated there, and the results were announced from the balcony. Most inns were deeply involved with elections, not only in providing refreshments and accommodation, but as premises where bribes could be passed and electors treated.

The entertainment to be found in the inns and taverns extended from informal and spontaneous outbursts of song to more organised events, which might take place in a first-floor concert room or dining-room. Billiards, bowls and skittles, may have been provided in many taverns, but have left few records. The Beverley Arms certainly had a purpose-built billiards room in the 1850s, and the Rose and Crown had one in the 1860s. Card games were permitted in public houses, but betting for money was totally forbidden. There are, however, many references in the brewsters' sessions' reports to landlords having permitted gambling on cards. When the landlord of the George and Dragon was charged with that offence in 1868 he denied it categorically, saying that a few tradesmen met for a hand of whist regularly but they did not play for money, though a magistrate found it difficult to believe. Some landlords organised cricket matches and others sporting events for their customers. Friendly societies were loyal to particular establishments for many years, and their social events centred around them.

Many, perhaps the majority, of the cases which came up at the regular police courts in the town involved people who had been drinking to excess. Drunkenness was certainly very common amongst all classes, but it was usually the lower classes who were censured for it. At corporation dinners numerous bottles of wine and spirits were consumed, and it was no uncommon thing for those members who had over-imbibed to be 'so drunk that they had to be taken home in a cab', a situation which was the subject of 'much chaffing' at a council meeting in 1858. In 1864 the landlady of the Blue Bell beerhouse was asked to describe the level of inebriation of one of her customers on Christmas Eve, when he had been drinking from 10 a.m. until 7 p.m. She described him as 'merry, and quite jolly, but not lushy'. She gave her definition of drunkenness as when a man could not stand up. However, by the Victorian period over-indulgence in alcohol was being perceived as a social problem by some people, and the temperance movement was one important response.

The temperance movement began in England in the 1820s as an attempt to reduce the consumption of spirits, which were very cheap and plentiful. An appeal for total abstinence was a natural progression of the movement's call for moderation. The early crusaders made much use of the oratorical methods and calls for conversion of the nonconformist revivalists, and the rejection of alcohol was closely related to the turning away from sin. It was recognised that merely advocating abstinence or moderation would have little appeal to the working man because so many activities were located in and around the public house. It would therefore be necessary to provide alternative recreations. Accordingly temperance and total abstinence societies soon put on full programmes of lectures, concerts, and tea parties, often in a purpose-built hall.

Beverley's Total Abstinence Society was established in December 1839 and was warmly welcomed by those elements in the town who yearned for a more respectable, serious, and well-educated society. It was particularly well-supported by the Primitive Methodists. The editor of the *Beverley Guardian* was a temperance advocate, which meant that the Society's activities were well (and favourably) reported.

The need for a hall for the Society's many activities was soon recognised, and in April 1845 a meeting was held to consider the matter. Subscriptions were promised and the following month negotiations were put in hand to purchase a piece of land in Well Lane, next door to the Baptist Chapel. The hall, which still remains (fig. 34), was soon erected, at a cost of £300, and provided premises for a wide range of activities. In 1855 the Society decided that members who lived near the Beck needed another hall, that at Well Lane being too far away. The new hall, in Holme Church Lane, was opened in April 1856 with a 'grand temperance revel' and a magic lantern show for the children.

Temperance societies' activities included 'missionary' work together with the provision of moral support and social and educational events for those who had signed the pledge. Outdoor meetings were the best way to gain new converts and took place from time to time in the Market Place and at Potter Hill, Beckside. The Society's programme consisted of lectures, tea meetings, concerts, and outdoor events such as galas and processions. The lectures were usually on the advantages of temperance, or the immorality of the drinks trade, or some allied topic. Lecturers came from all over the country, but particularly from the West Riding and Lancashire. One attraction of attending temperance lectures was the chance to hear reformed drunkards recounting their former lives in lurid detail. In 1867 such a man described his life as an orphan on the streets of London, and the 'trials and temptations' of a young man's life in the capital. The audience listened with 'deep emotion and breathless interest'. Recitations, songs, and a poem written about the signboards of Beverley's public houses followed. Some lecturers used humour or ridicule to make their point: much amusement was caused by the speaker, J. B. Gough, whose talk included imitations of drunkards, as well as the story of a Guardian of the Poor who 'had never known a teetotaller apply for relief in 22 years'.

Talks were given on literature, history, music , and religion, as well as upon the need for abstinence from strong drink. Music played a very important part in the programme. A temperance choir, a brass band, and a juvenile fife and drum band were formed and played at many events. Glees and madrigals as well as 'sweet temperance melodies' were often included in an evening's entertainment. In 1856 a Broadwood piano was bought for use in the hall. At Christmas, perhaps a time of particular temptation, the Society held a festival, including a sumptuous tea, and the evening's entertainment combined 'intellectual recreation and music'. The room was brightly decorated with mottoes, evergreens, flags, and, in 1856, 'allegorical paintings representing the millennium'. For the younger members of the Society a Band of Hope was instituted. Temperance children were often to be seen parading through the town. In February 1869, after such a procession, and a song around the Market Cross, almost 500 children sat down to tea in the hall. The temperance movement certainly had its positive aspects, and was closely associated with the drive for so-called 'rational recreations'.

CHAPTER EIGHT
OUTDOOR RECREATIONS

Beverlonians had many outdoor entertainments available to them throughout the year. As in the rest of the country there was in the town an increasing emphasis upon improving, educational, and health-giving activities, the so-called 'rational recreations', often sponsored by churches and chapels, educational societies or the temperance movement and intended to facilitate the mixing' of the classes, foster competition and promote local loyalties. Nevertheless the traditional festivities such as the Midsummer Fair, the commemoration of November 5th, and the statute hirings, were still celebrated with gusto. Beverlonians were also regularly entertained by the proceedings surrounding the election of their Members of Parliament and councillors.

Sporting activities included race meetings, cricket matches, athletic events, hunting, shooting and archery. The rougher sports and pastimes, such as football, bare-fisted boxing, cock-fighting, bull-baiting, badger-baiting, seem to have been diminishing or dying out completely. The Pits on Westwood were a suitable location for unofficial 'sports' meetings. Pitch and toss, alternatively called knurr and spell, dog fights, and bare-fisted boxing matches, all accompanied by betting, drew parties of young men there in the evenings. In 1861 a letter to the *Beverley Guardian* described a recent meeting for ratting on Westwood. A number of rats were put into a pit and a dog was thrown amongst them. None of the animals had any chance of escape until either the rats or the dog were killed. The onlookers, according to the correspondence, included 'the sons of clergymen, merchants, professional men, and even professional men themselves'. It was a sight which was 'surely ... not likely to add to the morality of the inhabitants of Beverley'.

Beverley was fortunate in possessing large open commons, and many more 'respectable' outdoor activities took place on Westwood (fig. 35), especially on the racecourse on Hurn, or in the 'sylvan retreat' of Burton Bushes, whose wide avenues provided an attractive location for tea parties and picnics, games, and sports of various kinds.

Race meetings had been taking place on Westwood since the late 17th century. In the mid-19th century the principal meeting took place in June, whilst a spring meeting incorporating a steeple chase was held in March or April in most years. There were several training stables in Beverley, most notably the establishment behind the Rose and Crown in North Bar Without. The facilities provided for racing in Beverley were good. Westwood itself provided an excellent ground, the oval course being almost a mile and a half, with a half mile straight run in. A grandstand had been built in the 1760s and was still being used in the mid-19th century (fig. 36). The commercial and trading interests of the town welcomed the business brought in by the race meeting.

Horse races were popular with all classes. They were sponsored by the gentry of the county, but the 'lower orders' were encouraged to attend to enjoy the spectacle and perhaps place a bet or two. The mixing of social groups which could occur was noted with approval by the local press. However such inter-mixing seems to have been limited. The ladies of the upper classes sat in the grandstand, well away from the 'rougher sex', and displayed their 'lovely smiling faces, ribbons and parasols' at a safe distance. On race day early in the morning the first excitement for people in the town was the race horses coming in by rail. A string of 39 horses was observed passing through the main streets by the *Beverley Guardian* reporter in 1856. The race meeting proper did not begin until early afternoon, but people began streaming onto Westwood much earlier. As the newspapers reported, Westwood in June presented 'a striking and beautiful appearance ... resplendent in buttercups and daisies' when 'crowds of gaily dressed pedestrians clambered the hills, descended the valleys, and emerged from the various outlets of its 'Bushy Pits' on their way to the ground'.

Meetings drew people from a wide radius around Beverley. In 1851 it was estimated that between five and six thousand people came from Hull, on trains laid on especially for the purpose. People also travelled by rail from York, Driffield, and Malton. Many came by road: the *Hull Advertiser* commented in 1850 upon the fact that every road-worthy vehicle available was utilised to transport people to Beverley races, including 'the carriage and pair (of dogs) of the crippled mendicant, the crack taxcart of the yeoman and the private carriage of the 'Man at Ease''.

Food and drink were provided from booths set up by traders from the town and from further afield. Many Beverley shopkeepers closed their premises on race days, thus allowing their employees a day's entertainment. Horse-racing brought together two of the Englishman's obsessions — horses and gambling — and book-makers attended in force. Business was described as 'very brisk', the 'stout yeomen of the East Riding' throwing their money around 'with great zest'.

Cricket was a very popular sport in Beverley in mid-Victorian times. The ground was near Black Mill on Westwood (fig. 37), and the miller, Mr. Wreghitt, apparently made himself responsible for the catering arrangements and for providing the spectators with music. Sometimes he entertained them himself on his cornet, with tunes chosen according to whether the home team was winning or losing. On other occasions he arranged for the brass band of the East Yorkshire Militia to play for the crowd. From 1859 he set up tents near the mill, one of them placed at a distance 'especially designed for the fair sex ... who graced the scene ... by a very numerous attendance to observe so fashionable a game'. The newspapers regarded the occasions with great approval, seeing them as well-organised and 'respectable' affairs.

Teams were drawn from a wide variety of backgrounds and occupations. The home team was the Beverley Amateur Cricket Club, which had at least two elevens in the 1850s. When they needed to add extra strength to their team they drew players from outside the town, as in August 1852, when an 'Eleven of All England' played Beverley and District. The match (won by All England) lasted several days, and cheap trains were put on to bring spectators into the town.

Teams from Hull often came to Beverley, and the ground was also used for matches between other villages. In July 1857 the *Beverley Guardian* recorded that numerous games had been played in the last few weeks:

> *We have had the Beverley and East Riding, the Beverlac, the Peep-o-Day Boys, the Break-o-Day Boys, the Mechanics, and the Rising Stars, but the match on Thursday last between two elevens, above 50 years of age was the one which produced the most excitement.*

Military teams appeared regularly. The Rifle Volunteers, formed in 1859, soon managed to muster a cricket team, and frequently played Beverley Amateurs in the 1860s. The youth of Beverley were also encouraged to form teams. In 1861 a match was played on Westwood 'between ten players selected by Master Sylvester [the mayor's son], and ten selected by Master Hodgson [the tanner's son]'.

Women were excluded from participating in most sports in the Victorian period. However, in the early 1860s, archery became popular amongst the upper and middle classes, and the *Beverley Guardian* noticed in 1865 that ladies had begun to take part. The society which organised the events, the East Yorkshire Archers, held its meetings in a field off Norwood. The contests lasted all day, punctuated by lunch provided by Francis Burrell of the White Horse. The band of the East Yorkshire Militia entertained the spectators, and at 7 p.m. the company moved to the Assembly Rooms, where the prizes were distributed, after which they danced to the Militia band.

So-called 'foot races' were very common in mid-century: in 1856 a Beverley man ran a mile in seven and a half minutes against an opponent from Bridlington. The milestone near Mount Pleasant on the York Road was the usual starting point for such races. On December 29 1860 the cricket ground near Black Mill was used for a 200 yard handicap foot race. The event was organised by the innkeeper of the Tanners' Arms, Keldgate.

At various times during the year people congregated on Westwood for games, sports and general recreations. Good Friday was a holiday, and if the weather were good large crowds of people, not only from Beverley but also from Hull and elsewhere, went there to enjoy themselves. A cricket match was usually organised, and music was provided for dancing or listening to. In 1854 a quadrille band played in Burton Bushes, and in 1864 and 1865 the brass bands of the Oddfellows and the Foresters entertained the crowds. At Easter 1865, perhaps encouraged by the popularity of those small-scale events, a group of townsmen decided to organise pony races and foot races on Hurn. Various worthies, including Beverley's M.P.s, put up small stakes. The grandstand and enclosure were open for the occasion (with the landlord of the Lion and Lamb 'making ample provision in the commissariat department') and refreshment booths were set up on the ground.

Friendly societies were well-supported in mid-century, and at that time the club feasts, which consisted of processions, followed by prolonged eating and drinking at favoured inns, were changing into more respectable occasions involving tea parties, games and sports. Several such events were held on

35   Westwood. (Humberside Arts and Leisure).

36   Race stand. (Beverley Race Committee).

Westwood in the 1850s and 1860s. On a Monday afternoon in September 1859, for example, the Independent Society organised a very popular fête in Burton Bushes. It began with a procession from the town, headed by the drum and fife band of the Temperance Society, and followed by a long line of children carrying banners, and one of Mr. Crathorne's waggons, full of children too small to walk so far. The *Beverley Guardian* reported that:

> *On arriving at their destination, the youngsters were regaled with refreshments, and a bountiful supply of pure spring water was conveyed thither in a barrel for the use of those who might need it. At no great distance from these were several tents, booths, and stalls, and in various convenient places were to be seen small tea parties, who with smiling faces seemed to do justice to that refreshing cup which cheers but does not inebriate. Others preferred a more stimulative beverage, and congregated at a large booth at the top of the grounds, where they quaffed their 'nut brown' and smoked their favourite weed in a truly independent manner, while a brass band at intervals enlivened the scene by its music. Dancing parties and kissing rings might have been observed in all directions ...*

A picnic on Westwood was the next best thing to an excursion to the seaside, and many children belonging to day schools and Sunday schools from Beverley and outside were taken by their teachers for a day out in Burton Bushes or the Pits. To make the occasion more memorable they often formed processions through the town, dressed in their best clothes, and preceded by brass bands. In June 1862 the Beverley Band of Hope and the children of the Sabbath School met the Hull Free Church Sabbath School children at the railway station, and all paraded through the streets and into Burton Bushes where they were organised for games. However not all children were in a position to dress up for treats: in 1852 a party of 74 children from Hull Ragged School came to Beverley by train. They walked in procession to the Market Cross, where they sang a hymn. Beverlonians' hearts were touched by the sight of so many children without shoes or stockings, and a subscription was raised to support the school funds and to accept contributions of clothes. The children went from the town onto Westwood where they played games, and then walked to the Temperance Hall for milk and spice buns.

The Primitive Methodists were very strong in Beverley in the Victorian period. An important aspect of their mission was making conversions via outdoor meetings. Westwood was an ideal venue, and camp meetings took place there every June attended by crowds of people, some of whom came not to participate but to heckle the preachers. A camp meeting in 1844 inspired a poem, when two old men who had come to make sport of the meeting, fell off the rail surrounding a pond into the water:

> *Two aged sires, whose limbs did fail,*
> *Sat down to rest upon a rail:*
> *I looked, and lo! the rail I found*
> *Did help to fence a pond around.*

These aged sires had lived so long,
And oft had joined the giddy throng;
They and their sins, be not surprised,
Had grown to a prodigious size.

They proved too heavy for the rail –
It broke, and headlong in they fell,
Some laughed aloud, while others cried:
'They're both converted and baptised!'.

(H. Woodcock, *Piety among the peasantry* (1889))

A growing source of interest in Beverley in the period was the military events which took place on Westwood and in the town streets. From 1852 the East Yorkshire Militia, which had only rarely been mustered since the end of the Napoleonic Wars, was raised again as a result of the Militia Act of that year. Previously troops had been raised by ballot, but from 1852 voluntary enlistment for five years replaced that system. In September 1852 a Militia recruiting party, accompanied by a fife and drum band, paraded the streets of Beverley. It was highly successful, for in October between three and four hundred men 'of a rather motley appearance' from the town and elsewhere in the East Riding, assembled on Westwood and were inspected by the officers. After being quartered on various publicans in the town they were drilled into some sort of order. The following May 700 men, the full complement, assembled in Beverley, where they were supplied with uniforms and trained three times daily on Westwood for three weeks, aided by a brass band. At the end of the training period a review of the Militia took place on the cricket ground near Black Mill, watched by 'more people than had ever been known on the Westwood at one time'. Those annual reviews became very popular with Beverlonians. A depot for the arms and stores was built in New Walk near the Sessions House. Behind it were houses for the permanent staff, and a training yard. A Militia brass band was soon formed and was called upon to play at many functions in the town. Their afternoon and evening concerts became regular events in the summertime, the band either playing in New Walk, in the Market Place, or outside the Beverley Arms.

In 1854 the Crimean War began, and soon the Militia were mustered in earnest and sent to Aldershot, where they remained until the end of the war in 1856, although some men volunteered to serve abroad and relieved regular soldiers on the battlefield. However by 1859 the initial enthusiasm for the Militia had waned, and only 200 of the required 900 attended the annual 21 days training. In that year, principally as a result of tension between Great Britain and France, the Government decided to establish a new organisation, the Volunteer Corps, soon to be known as the Rifle Volunteers because of their early adoption of the newly-invented rifle. Several companies were formed in the East Riding, the 6th (Beverley) Company being commanded by Captain Barkworth. In June 1860 at the annual review of the Militia, the Beverley Rifle Volunteers formed a guard of honour. A week later two Hull companies of Rifle Volunteers arrived at Beverley station, and, with the Beverley company, marched to the Westwood, where they gave a display to a large crowd.

Perhaps the greatest attraction of joining the Rifle Volunteers was the opportunity for rifle practice, and contests offering prizes were soon established. In November 1860 a cup valued at ten guineas, and a rifle valued at ten pounds were offered as prizes in a contest held on Westwood. Those shooting matches became regular events, and were keenly contested. Many people from the town went to watch, and refreshment tents were set up by local innkeepers.

The Rifle Volunteers met regularly for drill throughout the year, and frequently marched around the town and into the surrounding villages, preceded by their own brass band. In 1861 a Brigade field day was held on Westwood attended by companies from Hull, Bridlington, Driffield, Howden and Hedon. It was watched by thousands of spectators, many of them coming from Hull and district. The gentry of the area were well-represented, and tents were set up to provide a range of refreshments 'from ginger beer to the best French brandy'. Those military reviews became regular spectacles. East Yorkshire Militia reviews were the most colourful because the men wore scarlet tunics with white braid and white breeches (fig. 38). The Volunteers were drab in comparison, with grey tunics with black braid, red collars and cuffs, grey trousers with red stripes, and black leather belts (fig. 39). On the other hand the Volunteers corps had the rifles, and any review involving shooting was bound to draw a crowd. Old ladies were heard to remark that they had been to see the 'corpses' on parade, and 'Didn't the corpses look well today?'. *Punch* was less complimentary about the East Yorkshire Militia, calling them the East Chalkshires!

Market and fair days, more especially the latter, were important occasions for recreation. Beverley's market day was Saturday, and brought crowds of people in from all the surrounding villages. Stalls were set up in Saturday Market Place, country women sold produce from their baskets, and travelling dentists and patent medicine sellers did a good trade. The town had four fairs, mainly for the sale of horses, cattle, and sheep. The first (Candlemas) was held in February, the second on Ascension Day, the third (Midsummer Fair) in early July, and the fourth (Ringing Day Fair) in early November. Midsummer Fair and the November fair were also pleasure fairs, and the latter coincided with the statute hirings. Farm servants generally preferred to move around, and having received their year's wages, they went to the hirings held in all the East Riding towns, bought themselves new clothes, frequented the alehouses, enjoyed themselves at the amusements, and subsequently found for themselves new masters. For many of them it was their only real holiday in the whole year. Beverley had its hirings in early November, at old Martinmas. The country people took great pains with their dress when they came into the town:

> *the chief portion of the male sex showing their best black to great advantage, the bottoms of their trousers being turned up for displaying the pains they had bestowed on a pair of well blacked boots. The neck ties, too, could not fail to attract attention on account of their being tastily tied, each evidently striving to arrange his dress to give entire satisfaction to his lady-love, who*

127

37   Cricket match (Black Mill), c.1860. (East Yorkshire Borough of Beverley Borough Council).

38   Band Sergeant Arthur Pearson, East Yorkshire Militia, c.1862. Photo by Winter and Son,
Beverley. (East Yorkshire Borough of Beverley Borough Council).

as neat and clean as a new pin, in her crinoline, was hanging on his arm, and his 'endeavours to please must have been crowned with success' when her bewitching smile met his view.

Women too were hired at the sittings, and in the late 1850s the sight of females standing on street corners or in public houses, waiting to be chosen, offended the Victorian sense of propriety, so a number of townspeople, including several clergymen and ladies, arranged for the Assembly Rooms to be used to hire female servants in seclusion. Refreshments were provided, improving books were on sale, and business was brisk: in 1862 the number passing through the doors was about 2,000, and 1,400 were inside at one time.

That attempt to make hiring day more respectable was a response to the natural high spirits displayed by some of the 'gaily dressed rustics', who were determined to enjoy their scant holiday time to the full. A reporter from the *Hull Advertiser* recorded in 1853 with satisfaction that he was 'glad to observe that drunkenness and rioting is very markedly on the decrease at the fairs, and particular at the last one'. The hirings at Beverley seem to have been quite law-abiding occasions. The Midsummer Fairs too were becoming more well-ordered than hitherto, when drunkenness was rife. A newspaper account of 1863 tells of an earlier time when it was 'almost a point of honour, or rather dishonour, for the 'lovers of lush' to get drunk ... but time works wonders, which Monday last gave strong proof, for we do not remember seeing fewer drunkards in the streets'. The same commentator also noted that there were now rival attractions to the fairs for country folk:

> *In regard to country visitors, there was a decided falling off, the decrease being especially in reference to bonny lads and handsome lasses, in gay attire, being plainly visible. The spread of education, combined with religious instruction, has done much to improve the moral condition of the rural population. Honest John and modest Mary, who hope shortly to become man and wife, are apparently more refined in their pursuit of pleasure, preferring rather to avail themselves of numerous cheap excursions to look with wonderment on the beautiful works of Creation, than to travel for miles through dust and dirt to witness what they have so often seen before.*

In 1864 another newspaper made a similar point, observing that:

> *The attendance of country visitors was very small indeed, there not being so many as have been seen on some market days, which plainly indicated that pleasure fairs in this part of the country are fast dying out, the rural population preferring those rational recreations placed within their reach by cheap excursion trains to travelling to a town where they had so often been before for the purpose of patronising noise and confusion.*

That view may be somewhat biased, and betray a certain wishful thinking on the part of the middle class elements in the town, who tended to frown upon the few occasions for jollity that were available to the hard-working country people.

The Midsummer and November fairs seem to have been a satisfactory mixture of business and pleasure. The horses were displayed in North Bar Within, and when buying was in full swing there the scene was not only noisy but hazardous, as passers-by might find themselves bitten or kicked by nervous animals. The northern part of the Market Place, the Sow Hill section, was devoted to the sale of all sorts of agricultural requirements, such as rakes, forks, scythes, and wheel spokes, with 'ling besoms by the thousands'. Those brooms, sand stones for sharpening scythes, and bundles of herbs, were brought to Beverley by hawkers from the North Riding, described by the *Beverley Guardian* as 'that queer, hardy, gipsey-like looking race who inhabit the moors beyond Pickering'. Ginger bread sellers and lollipop sellers, with boxes of sweets suspended from their shoulders, did a good trade here. In another part of the Market Place were stalls selling women's clothing, caps and corsets, bonnets, ribbons and kerchiefs, and there were hardware and oyster stalls, and people selling nuts and oranges. Standing on or near the Market Cross, and attracting a large crowd, might be a smooth-talking 'Cheap John who entertained a large party in front of his van in spinning long and humorous yarns in praise of his articles ...' or 'an eloquent worm doctor who could worm a 6d out of your pocket and would promise to cure you of all the ills that flesh is heir to' (fig. 40). Also around the Cross were 'what is called Bazaars, furnished with all sorts of toys for young and old. And organs were droning out their several sounds, and fiddles were squeaking, and ballad singers were at their vocation'. But for the youngsters Corn Hill, the section of the Market Place in front of the Corn Exchange, must have been the centre of attraction. Here were placed the swing boats and roundabouts, 'which even to look upon made the most staid and circumspect and slow as giddy as a goose'. In that area too were shooting galleries, each adorned with 'a fancy front, which could not fail to please the eye, ... and smiling young ladies who had charge of them [but] were not so active as they wished to be', and booths containing persons of 'unusually large and small dimensions, and persons professing the Black Art'. In 1864 one of the exhibitions was 'of so disgusting a character, a fellow devouring live rats, that after a few performances on Saturday night, the proprietor very properly received notice from the Mayor to quit'. The travelling shows which visited a provincial town were not generally on a large scale. In 1857 'a learned pig, accompanied by a Caledonian youth weighing upwards of 500 pounds, a glass-blowing exhibition, and a peep-show' were the most impressive attractions, and in 1859:

> *The show department was miserably represented, and the clowns the most imperfect specimens we ever saw or heard ... The proprietor of one of the principal shows, named Swallow, announced that his establishment was a 'circus', but his stud was on a very limited scale, as there was only a pony, and the chief equestrian was a monkey. His neighbour ... astonished not a few of the natives, with the inexhaustible bottle trick, besides performing the rather ungallant feat of 'extinguishing' a young lady. One thing very remarkable was the entire absence of those*

time-honoured exhibitions called 'peep shows', upon extensive
fronts of which were generally illustrated sanguinary battles and
the latest novelty in the murder line, but their places were well
supplied with blowing machines called 'expirators' at which a
rustic might have been seen trying the strength of his lungs till he
was nearly black in the face, while a companion standing near,
told him to take care, or he would 'brust his biler'...

It seems to have been a required part of the day's entertainment on fair day
for the young country people to climb up one of the Minster towers to look at
the view. Some people were not satisfied with making the ascent once: a
'buxom-looking lass was overheard to say, whilst talking to her lover,
perchance, 'That she had been to the top of the steeple four times that morning,
and if he would only go with her she would go up again', to which he readily
assented'.

The circuses and menageries which occasionally came to the town were on a
somewhat larger scale than the travelling shows. A procession with loud music,
brightly decorated horses and waggons, and, best of all, exotic animals such as
elephants, lions, tigers, and apes, must have caused a sensation. In mid-
Victorian times there was a multiplicity of circuses travelling the country. Many
of them consisted predominantly of equestrian acts. Menageries, or circuses
including foreign animals, caused the most excitement. The account from the
Beverley Guardian of 1860 describing the arrival of Mander's menagerie is
worth quoting:

This large establishment came into the town in procession on
Tuesday last, headed by a very elegant carriage drawn by three
camels and two horses, which contained an excellent brass band,
Maccomo, the celebrated African lion hunter, being the driver.
The whole 'turn-out' to say the least of it, was a highly
respectable affair, and drew together a large number of
spectators, who much admired the beautiful horses attached to
the different caravans. The black-maned lion, Nero, together
with the lioness, Victoria, and her young ones, commanded their
due share of attention, while the tigers ... were much admired ...
Maccomo astonished the company by his daring feats with the
lions and tigers, and the command he had over them ... was truly
surprising, as a mere wave of his hand was all that was required to
put these striped animals through their evolutions.

Maccomo the lion tamer was considered one of the most daring men of the
age with wild beasts. Many expected him to die a violent death, but he died of
natural causes in 1870. Perhaps courage was not always required of lion-
tamers. In April 1862 Sanger's circus and menagerie entered Beverley. It was
recorded of one of Sanger's lions that it was 'so tame that it used to be taken
from the cage to impersonate the British lion, lying at the feet of Britannia, in
the cavalcades customary with tenting circuses when entering a town'.

Circuses, which required plenty of space, used fields near the town. In 1851
Hengler's circus entertained in a pavilion set up in a field near North Bar, whilst

39   Unknown Rifle Volunteer, 1868. (Roy Wilson).

40   Saturday Market Place. Luke Clennell, c.1835. (East Yorkshire Borough of Beverley Borough Council).

in 1856 performances of Macarte's circus took place in a marquee erected in a paddock at the back of the Beverley Arms. In 1858 the same paddock was used by Pablo Fanque's circus. In 1860, 1861, and 1862 Howe's and Cushing's American circus came to the town, bringing not only equestrians and acrobats, but also the renowned mules, Pete and Barney, and the famous American bull, Don Juan. Boxing matches, including 'the celebrated Tom Sayers', were part of the attractions at that circus. Chipperfield's Exhibition, including the Living Skeleton,was crowded with spectators when it came in 1864, many people having a second interview with 'this special representative of skin and bone'.

A recital of the indoor and outdoor recreations of Beverley in the mid-Victorian period might give an impression of a town bursting with life and activity. That would be a false picture. Certainly Beverlonians did have their excitements — the races, the Midsummer Fair, the Militia and Rifle Volunteers' reviews, a circus visit, concerts and panoramas, galas on Westwood, the odd cricket match or running race — but those were highlights in an otherwise uneventful calendar. A visitor to Beverley, Edwin Waugh, in the 1860s, only noticed the sleepiness of the town in the early summertime:

> *My short sojourn at the old town of Beverley left many pleasing pictures upon my memory; and it was a beneficial change to body and mind. And it was not until I got to the railway station, amongst the bustle of trains, and tickets, and trucks, and corduroy-clad porters, that I felt that I was waking to the life of the nineteenth century again.*

POSTSCRIPT

The mid-Victorian period has been labelled the 'Age of Equipoise', a period of relative calm and stability when the majority of the population was able to live in sociable harmony. It is a term which matches well the even tenor of life in Beverley in mid-century. For a time in the late 1860s the town had brought itself to national attention when its name became synonymous with bribery and corruption, but for the most part Beverley remained undisturbed by great events. Its preoccupations were almost entirely local. Even at the parliamentary elections little interest was displayed in national affairs. Yet it was affected by some of the same problems and preoccupations that affected other parts of the country. Clark's report on the public services of the town shows that problems of sewage disposal, a polluted water supply, and poor housing were not confined to the larger towns and cities. Throughout the mid-Victorian period the council invariably responded to such problems by applying short-term remedies; their solution was left to the 1870s and 1880s when water and sewage schemes were implemented.

Reflected in the pages of the *Beverley Guardian* and the *Beverley Recorder* is the concern with self-help and self-improvement which was so characteristic of the Victorians. The impression given that Beverley was becoming a more 'respectable' place may be in part the result of wishful thinking by the reporters. Nevertheless the many recreational activities in the town which were geared towards self-improvement provide evidence of the desire for education among many Beverlonians. At the same time there existed a sub-culture of working-class life in the town which was rarely reported in the pages of the newspapers, except when it resulted in the breaking of the law. Such social bias is one of the deficiences of newspapers as a source; another is the political bias inevitable when one newspaper was staunchly Conservative and the other fiercely Liberal. Nevertheless the hardest part of compiling this study has been that of selecting from the wealth of material to be found in those newspapers.

SELECT SOURCES

The Humberside County Archives Office holds the records of Beverley Borough Council and Beverley Poor Law Union. It also has records relating to churches, chapels, the Assembly Rooms, and various clubs and societies. Beverley Local History Library has an excellent collection of published works relating to the town. The list below is restricted to the more important sources used.

Primary sources

Census for Beverley for the years 1851 and 1861.
Beverley Guardian, 1856-1870.
Beverley guide: being a short account of the principal objects of the town. Beverley: John Kemp, 1847.
Beverley Recorder, 1856-1870.
Hull Advertiser, 1840-1855.
Ordnance Survey Map 1:1,056 Beverley, sheets 1-5. 1853 edition.
Sheahan, J. J. *Green's ... hand-book to Beverley*, c. 1875.
Sheahan, J. J. *and* Whellan, T. *History and topography of the City of York ... and the East Riding*, 1855.
Ward's Almanacks, 1860-70.
Waugh, Edwin. 'An old nest', *in his*: *Rambles in the Lake Country and other sketches*, c. 1865.
White, F. and Co. *General directory and topography of Kingston upon Hull and the City of York*, 1851, 1858, and 1867.
White, Walter. *A month in Yorkshire*, 1859.

Secondary sources

Ainley, A. N. 'Public elementary education in Beverley, East Yorkshire, 1840-1902'. Leeds University M.Ed. thesis, 1977.
Allison, K. J., *ed. A history of the County of York, East Riding.* Volume 6: *Beverley*, 1989.
Brown, A. 'William Spencer: his influence on Wesleyan education in Beverley, 1848-1887'. Hull University M.Ed. dissertation, 1983.
Brown, G. M. 'Endowed middle class education in Beverley'. Hull University M.Ed. dissertation, 1983.
Brown, Philip. *Old Beverley*, 1983.
MacMahon, K. A. *Beverley*, 1973.
Markham, John. 'Elections and electioneering in East Yorkshire, with particular reference to Hull and Beverley, 1815-1865'. Hull University M.A. thesis, 1976.
Markham, John, *ed. Philip Brown's Beverley*, 1990.
Wainwright, C. 'The Mechanics' Institute movement with particular reference to Hull and Beverley'. Hull University M.A. dissertation, 1984.